BEING AND NOT BEING

O. Weininger

BEING AND NOT BEING

Clinical Applications
of the Death Instinct

O. Weininger

Foreword by
Michael Eigen

INTERNATIONAL UNIVERSITIES PRESS, INC.
Madison   Connecticut

First published in 1996 by
H. Karnac (Books) Ltd.
58 Gloucester Road
London SW7 4QY

Library of Congress Cataloging-in-Publication Data

Weininger, Otto, 1929–
    Being and not being : clinical applications of the death instinct
/ O. Weininger ; foreword by Michael Eigen.
        p.   cm.
    Includes bibliographical references and index.
    ISBN 0-8236-0465-9
    1. Death instinct.   2. Parent and Child.   3. Psychoanalysis.
I. Title.
BF175.5.D4W45   1996
155.9'37—dc20   96-25097
                                                                  CIP

Manufactured in the United States of America

CONTENTS

PART TWO
Manifestations in our community

ACKNOWLEDGEMENTS

I want to thank Mary Morris for so generously helping me organize this book. With her critical reading of the text, she has brought a greater clarity to my writing.

Christina Whyte-Earnshaw has been very giving of her time by reading and commenting upon the revised manuscript. Virginia Cooper has reviewed the manuscript from a sensitive and discriminatory point of view.

I am indebted to others: to Dan Blais and Nancy Solomon, who have kindly and consistently helped me to complete the book, and to Joyce Townsend for her work in preparing the manuscript.

Sylvia Singer, my wife, has been an important support to me and my work for a long time now. I am grateful to her for putting up with me while I was thinking through ideas and then writing them down.

I also want to thank my patients and my students; it is with them that I learn.

PREFACE

I n this book I attempt to unravel some of the mysteries of
our early emotional development, in particular, the process
whereby some of us get so angry, yet others cannot become
angry at all, and the reasons why some of us have such a strong
urge to destroy people and things, yet others have such a problem recognizing their own or others' destructive feelings. I
believe there is in all of us a balance to destroy and to protect,
but in some of us the balance is tilted too far in one direction.

Editorial note

For the sake of simplicity, all unidentified children are referred
to in the masculine throughout this text.

FOREWORD

Michael Eigen

"I believe there is in all of us a balance to destroy and to protect, but in some of us the balance is tilted too far in one direction." So says Dr. Otto Weininger at the beginning of this work. No problem is more important for our age. What enables a life to be predominantly constructive rather than destructive for self and world? What can psychoanalysis do to tip the balance for the better?

Dr. Weininger cuts through jargon to give many clear and useful portrayals of work with destructive tendencies in a variety of contexts. He has much to say about adults who seem to stall or live life in reverse. There are many individuals who feel numb or dead and undo whatever they try to build. Dr. Weininger shares his attempts to contain the pain of unlived or mislived lives and provide psychic nutrients that make constructive aliveness possible.

Dr. Weininger's book is rich in nutrients for the reader, also. Not only does he have helpful things to say about destructive processes in adults, but his book contains a wealth of material on work with children. He traces death work to its sources in early feeding and sleeping problems, various somatic difficulties, phenomena like homesickness, and crises of spirit that disabled and dying children must face.

His portrayal of the importance of the emotional and attitudinal atmosphere of institutional and medical care in face of a child's terminal illness sensitizes us to the crucial battle of spirit that goes on in the interplay of individuals at all levels of life. In one instance, a hospital could not tolerate a youngster pinning a picture on the wall, so fearful was it of losing its own undamaged state in face of the massive psychophysical damage its charges underwent. The damaged child may try to get from an institution the protection his parents could not give. How often our own damaged selves are unable to respond to the call of those who need us most!

Dr. Weininger points out that a good emotional atmosphere can even make medication work more effectively, even in the face of death. In one instance, an ill baby began responding to medication after three nurses took a real interest in him. He began responding to the responsive nurse. His ability to respond came alive so that he could begin to use other elements in the caregiving situation. Dr. Weininger felt "it was the attachment he was able to form to his caregivers that gave him the needed security and safety to continue living". That life calls to life is not merely blind faith. The psychological atmosphere we breathe in can affect whether we live or die, whether we flourish.

Dr. Weininger is not reductive in his depiction of destructive processes. He calls attention to the role unconscious phantasy plays in magnifying annihilation dread, sometimes rendering ameliorating contact difficult and impossible. At the same time, he points to mutual permeability, the real effects we have on each other. We need to support each other in life, to support emotional aliveness. Without psychological care, we die out or become monstrous mangled versions of ourselves.

All too often, coming alive emotionally may be indistinguishable from destructiveness and seem ugly or repulsive, if we are not used to it. Too often we recoil from each other's growth in aliveness, sometimes in horror, but sometimes because it is bothersome and demanding. Dr. Weininger points out how difficult it can be to switch to a child's time world, and give the time needed to let a child's impact speak to one. One may or may not agree with what the child wants or how it goes about getting it.

But one can taste, even savour the impact, let the prismatic reflections spread, let the child know you know he is alive, that you are alive to him. We do not have to hide from our own or each other's aliveness, and live with more than one foot in the grave.

This book is an eloquent plea for life, for emotional aliveness, for the possibility of living well together. It points out what can happen when a wide range of feelings have no place in real living. We choke on and swallow ourselves, drop into a deadness worse than death, initiate destructive actions that deaden ourselves more, become dangerous not only to ourselves, but to the social fabric, just as destructive elements in the social fabric are dangerous to us. To what extent can we turn things around?

In one instance, a child felt he needed 20 sweet rolls from Dr. Weininger before he could say, "My insides are really good now." The more than 20 examples of meeting destruction with understanding aliveness that abound in this book make our insides better too.

PART ONE

CLINICAL
MANIFESTATIONS

Early developmental origin of the death instinct: its relationship to the superego

Young infants, even as young as 3 months of age, are quite capable of showing anger and rage, usually seen by flailing their arms, kicking their legs, screaming, grimacing, and holding their breath (Lewis, 1995; Oster & Ekman, 1978). Parents have often commented to me about their baby's anger, usually along with the statement—"I don't really think that a baby so young is able to show anger." However, sometimes they questioned their own statements of disbelief about their baby's feelings, because they brought up several other instances where the baby showed what they thought were "grown-up feelings".

> I was watching a 10-month-old baby, whose father left her in order to answer the telephone. After he left the room, she usually searched for him, looking all around the room from her play seat. When she was unable to locate him, her face and the corners of her mouth began to droop, her eyes narrowed and, in closing, appeared to droop as well. Generally, her whole body seemed to take up less space than before. When the father returned in a few minutes, he went

over to greet her and picked her up. Her body seemed to be very loose and floppy, without the muscle tone she had first evidenced before his brief absence. When he talked to her, she did not look at him and turned away from his look, and for what was probably an instant appeared to me to be angry. She then turned to look at him with a wide grin and smile, and father responded with an equally bright grin and vocal greetings; they resumed their play, and daughter responded.

There was, however, an interruption in the relationship brought on by the father's departure. I think the child was angry and experienced the anger. While it was painful, it was not so disruptive as to have any lasting quality. Perhaps the baby's anger was a result of a change in the comfortable state she experienced when father was present; he was communicating with her, and she seemed to gain much pleasure from this, as shown by her gleeful vocalizations, her smiles, and her touching his face. When he suddenly left, this pleasure was also removed, and her anger was focused on father.

At 10 months, babies are able to associate their sense of uncomfortableness with the actions of others (Emde, Gaesbauer, & Harmon, 1976). Babies are now able to express anger as a response to the behaviour of their parents. They express anger and rage when the parent does not respond appropriately, is unresponsive, and does not seem to care, is unavailable for nurturing or is disappointing in giving affection. Such babies feel empty and experience a sense of not being—a sense of death.

An 8-month-old boy who had been sucking his thumb seemed to be content, yet he suddenly began to scream loudly and kick at his parent when the parent came over to pick him up. I wondered whether the baby's apparent contented state was disrupted because the baby was left alone too long or was hungry. When the parent did not appear "on time", the baby responded with anger, perhaps even leading to a sense of not being valued. Babies do need to be picked up, talked to, and played with. When parents say, "I think he's content to be by himself, I'll just leave him alone for a while longer", perhaps they are misjudging the amount of time the baby wants to be alone.

In the above example, the baby's anger was directed at the parent. As the parent was able to calm the baby by talking to him and gradually gathered him to be picked up, the baby's expression became one of pleasure and responsiveness. The baby's anger was tolerated by this parent who had no need to make the baby "feel badly" for being angry, no matter what was the cause.

> Anger is again illustrated in another infant of 7 months, who began to cry loudly and kick when his parent tried to pick him up. However, in this situation the parent began to tell the infant that he should be satisfied and not be so angry, because if he continued to be angry, he would not be fed. The parent continued, "You have everything you need, and I won't spoil you by giving in to your every whim." This baby did not stop crying for about 30 minutes, but when he did become calm, he refused to feed. This baby's anger was not tolerated, and, I think, the baby was made to feel very anxious in relationship to his parent. In a way, I think that in refusing to feed, the baby tried to disown his feelings, perhaps of anger, even though it seemed more as if the baby was rejecting the need for food. The baby seemed to be in the process of disowning feelings and needs that he experienced as being frightening.

Babies learn how to protect themselves by disowning feelings that are not valued, that are rejected, or that cause reactions in others that are felt by the babies as leaving them with a sense of nothingness, of not being anyone, of being bad. Shame, in this way, is the response of the baby to the parent as a persecuting person. I think the baby's experience of shame, of being bad, is the result of the parent forcing the baby to cope with unpleasant, discomforting realities for which the baby is as yet maturationally unprepared or to which the baby has other responses, such as anger. Shame in babies and young children is their emotional response to parental blocking of aggression and anger. Crittenden (in press) points out:

> Infants exhibit individual differences in their sense of self that emerges from their relationships with caregivers. That is, in the context of their caregivers' response to them, in-

fants experience some feelings more often and more in-
tensely than others and, more importantly, come to feel more
or less competent to move from one feeling state to another
without experiencing discouraging periods of distress. Depending upon the responsiveness of their caregivers they
also feel more or less comfortable with their feeling states,
more or less recognized by their caregivers, and more or less
competent to communicate with their caregivers. Infants
who are left to cope alone with distress may come both to
fear feelings and also to dislike the self that has such feelings. [p. 10]

Certainly the care that babies are given will affect the way in
which they feel about themselves. Infants who are given good
enough responses by their parents come to feel good enough
about themselves. Infants who are ignored, rejected, or abused
seem to be unable to feel comfortable with their feelings. Some
babies may even not want anything and have little capacity to
recognize that they can gain some nurturance. Such babies fail
to thrive. Some other babies seem to be unable to become
pleased or satisfied—as if satisfaction were bad. These babies
disown their feelings, particularly those feelings that make them
sense that their world is a dangerous place. In these babies, any
feeling like aggression, anger, satisfaction, pleasure, and even
love is disowned; their reactions to their parents and others are
only those reactions that are felt to be "safe ones"—that is, those
emotions that will not result in being ignored, rejected, or
abused.

Being ignored, rejected, or abused also makes the baby feel
angry, but the anger must be dissociated, not even felt. For, if it
is expressed or felt, then the baby's own sense of badness is
increased. The parent supports this sense of badness by ignor-
ing or punishing or rejecting the baby for its feelings once again.
So anger must be avoided, because it will only make a bad
situation worse, resulting in less "love and care" with less and
less goodness for the baby to "take in". The parents are seen as
controlling people, and the baby must conform or be rejected.
Conformity might mean "love", but expressing anger will result
in dangerous rejection. In this way our fear of badness is our
fear of being annihilated by the very people who are to care for
us—our parents become our persecutors. We must avoid the

punishment directed towards ourselves by the parents (Suttie, 1935).

These babies develop very harsh and severe superegos. The superego begins to develop within the pregenital phase and originates in, and is governed by, the very early destructive impulses. The anxiety created by the power of the destructiveness is phantasized as overwhelming or annihilating the baby. The defence against this destruction is to spur the superego formation in ways that will counter in some way these early destructive impulses.

The superego, developed by introjection and oral cathexis of the primary external objects, is related to the extent and quality of the projections made by the baby to these external objects. The superego thus formed is both independent of, and yet intimately related to, the external objects. The ways these real external objects react will have a significant effect upon the workings of the introjected model and, therefore, upon the workings of the baby's superego (Weininger, 1992).

The strength of the superego is felt by the baby when, in expressing certain feelings, a sense of annihilation results. Emotional needs for nurturance and safety, emotional expressions of anger and satisfaction, even love, are experienced by such babies as bad, with resulting severe feelings of discomfort, muscle tension, and generalized anxiety. It is as if these babies sense that they are wanting too much, expressing too much, and that rejection as annihilation and as punishment will be forthcoming. The superego controls these expressions in the baby. The anxiety of expressing strong emotions occurs because of the anticipated parental disapproval, coupled with the phantasy of punishment from the internal parental object.

The real objects behind those imaginary, terrifying figures are the child's own parents, and those dreadful shapes in some way or other reflect the features of its father and mother, however distorted and phantastic the resemblance may be (Klein, 1933, p. 249).

The distortion is a consequence of the child's own aggressive impulses projected to the parents and then feared as attacking him with just the same anger as he attacks them for real or imagined hurts, pains, and frustrations. Now the baby fears for its own life. If the parent is unresponsive or rejecting, the infant has no other way of reacting to the specific behaviour than to feel that he has been doing something really bad and is now being punished. However, the punishment comes not only from the real parent but also from the infant itself, for it is the infant who, while reacting to the parent's response, must perceive itself as having done something bad or felt something wrong to which the parent is now reacting. It is, I think, the baby's internal conflict over damaging or destroying the parents, with the consequent masochistic behaviour of not thriving, not feeling, and not being able to think any more (Segal, 1957).

The harshness of the superego thus formed is, then, the loud voice of the death instinct, the loud sound of the sense of ego annihilation. It is the beginnings of a sense of dislike for the self, a self that is felt to be bad and always in danger of becoming annihilated and destroyed because of the badness that is being expressed by feelings and needs.

Let us now look at some of the different kinds of parent/infant relationships and how these affect what the infant learns about his feelings and needs and how these affect superego development in the child.

Some infants, whose parents are supportive, containing, predictable, and responsive, learn that their needs will be taken care of effectively, and their sense of taking too much or projecting their bad feelings will not result in unsupportive parents. These infants, when they become angry, do not stay angry for long. Rather, their ego develops in such a way as to perceive and recognize the goodness of their parents and their containing capacities. The infant's superego development is such that inwardly directed aggression is slight, the ego having been supported and now capable of more accurately interpreting the parent's continued goodness. The infants do not phantasize a state of no dependency nor no nurturing, and their superegos are not harsh. The death instinct is less severe with less anxiety about being destroyed by another and therefore less destructiveness directed towards the self. Needs, feelings, and satisfaction are not dangerous to sense and experience. Anticipatory phantasies are part of such babies lives, and for them the anticipation of satisfaction is not full of terror.

The meaning that some other infants learn to give to their feelings of anger and rage is that their parents do respond to their emotional states, but they do so too quickly. These parents do not seem able to set up an "emotional dialogue" with their babies. They do not wait to recognize how their babies will respond but react and respond immediately. This lack of communication gives the babies the sense of a parental response without understanding, without "taking in the babies' feelings", "without thinking". These babies stay angry for a long time, and the parents do not seem to understand why the babies are so distressed. They maintain unawareness of the nature of their babies' difficulties and distress. It is almost as if the parents think that to recognize the babies' feelings might make the parents aware of a feeling of being unable to cope with the distress. It is, I think, an avoidance of their own sense of inadequacy in parenting. Such parents may be very solicitous, even over-protective, yet they cannot cope with their babies' anger. They seem to have a lot of difficulty in calming their babies.

I think that in these babies the anger triggers a superego response that is extreme in quality and degree and that makes the babies perceive the environment as continually dangerous. The danger is that emotional expressions will annihilate. Anger is bad because the parent has not been able to make the baby feel better. The parent has communicated anger as bad because the parent has responded so quickly to the emotion without trying to take into account what may have occasioned the anger. Even if the parent does not know why the baby is angry, talking to the baby and expressing one's own sense of wanting to help is a first step in alleviating the painful feeling of anger. However, in this situation, the parent has communicated to the baby (by a rapid and undifferentiated response to anger) an anxious sense that it is bad to be angry.

The environment is also perceived as "dangerous" because it becomes very limiting due to the fact that the infant does not learn how to examine its feelings or how to explore its developing self. These infants become dependent and often overly "good" babies in response to their sense that their feelings are bad and must be controlled. For these infants, anger becomes the trigger for the superego to enter and control feelings, if not behaviours. The harshness of the superego will be exhibited by an over-exaggerated goodness on the part of these infants. The superego control may become so strong that it results even in an "extreme deadliness in which the parent seems to be drawn towards death and oblivion" (Steiner, 1981).

The interplay between the superegos of the infant and the ego of the parent creates, I think, a sense of not being in the infant, where the expression of nurturing—both to give to and to receive affection from the infant—become narrow and controlled. On the parent's side, the affection quality from the infant is never felt as good enough, and on the infant's side, expressions of gaining nurturance for needs and feelings are experienced as bad.

I have spoken with a number of parents who have expressed the feeling that they do not know how to nurture their infants. Their infants do not seem able to make use of the nurturing. They fail to thrive, even though their food intake is adequate (Valenzuela, 1989). When presented with an understanding and caring person, who helps to maintain a feeling of adequacy in the parent, particularly to cope with their baby's non-expressive behaviour, the sense of non-being in both is changed. The parental reaction to the baby's behaviour is no longer the same, and the reality begins to alter the baby's phantasy of the need to be overly good (Weininger, 1989). The content of the phantasies of annihilation and destruction are influenced by the nurturing experiences with the parent.

Other babies learn that a different meaning should be given to their feelings of anger. These are the babies who are ignored and whose anger or distress does not bring support or responsive care from the parents, or the babies who are abused because of the expression of feelings. These are the babies who learn to predict that their emotional states result in no care and/or in rejection and abuse. These babies quickly learn to try to do everything for themselves and in time do not tolerate easily any intrusions into their own contained worlds. They continue to be angry children, and aggression is triggered when their way of being is interrupted or when their needs become so unbearable that they cannot satisfy themselves. This aggression is directed unconsciously at the parent but only serves to make their perceived world even more dangerous (Weininger, 1992). Now there is the anxiety of retaliation, and the harshness of the superego is expressed by curtailing expressions of feeling. Emotions are only expressed when intense, and this situation creates an atmosphere of intense danger for the infant. The harshness of the superego is triggered in an attempt to prevent the expression of feelings that are felt to lead to annihilation from the other. These babies experience parental anger and rejection, which can only be felt as punishment, as a disintegrating force, and as annihilation—the death instinct. These infants learn to inhibit their feelings—and seem to react as if things are all right. In reality things are not all right, because these infants feel rejected, especially if they show emotions.

In summary, babies will experience their anger in ways that correspond to the ways parents respond to their anger. The early and harsh superego is not, however, simply the incorporation of parental values, but is also based upon their own phantasies of sadism and destructiveness to their parents. Their aggression and anger is frightening to themselves, and more so when the parents respond to these feelings with rejection or abuse. The harshness of the superego is not only to protect them from expressing anger and subsequent rejection, but also to protect the ego from death and annihilation (Suttie, 1935; Weininger, 1992, 1993). The infant must try to preserve itself, must prevent its death. The anxiety that the infant experiences is from the "operation of the death instinct within the organism, which is experienced as a fear of annihilation" (Klein, 1958, p. 84). The death instinct, then, as Rosenfeld describes it, is "a primary anxiety in the infant related to the fear of death" (Rosenfeld, 1990, p. 127).

CHAPTER TWO

Developmental origins of the death instinct: children's phantasy contributions to the harshness of superego formation

"Sometimes I get so mad—I could just get so mad that I'd die" a girl of 10 years said during one of her play psychotherapy sessions, as if she felt she would lose control of life. "Self-preservation implies an effort against some source of disintegration; the affective aspect of this is fear, fear of death"

[Zilboorg, 1943, p. 467]

I think it is very difficult for children to understand, and to cope with, not only their feelings about dying, but also their feelings about anger and sometimes about love. These feelings are very strong and intense, and often the young child's ego capacity is not sufficient to handle the strength of these emotions.

"The child who has good maternal experiences will develop a sense of basic security and will not be subject to morbid fears of losing support, of being annihilated, or the like" (Becker, 1973, p. 13). However, feelings are intensified, not only by conflict and by the playing out of relationships within the child's family, but also by relationships within the child's unconscious phantasy. The difficulty is also compounded by the superego—the young child's sense of guilt at perceiving its own greed and aggression directed towards the parent or the combined couple.

> In a magical world where things cause other things to happen just by a mere thought or look of displeasure, anything can happen to anyone. When the child experiences inevitable and real frustrations from his parents, he directs hate and destructive feelings toward them; and he has no way of knowing that malevolent feelings cannot be fulfilled by the same magic as were his other wishes. He thus has no real control over the magical cause and effect that he senses, either inside himself or outside in nature and in others: his destructive wishes could explode, his parents' wishes likewise. [Becker, 1973, p. 18]

Klein's suggestion of the earlier development of the superego provided her with the understanding that the death instinct is not silent, as Freud had hypothesized. Klein's observations of young children and her clinical work with them provided her with evidence, not only of the early beginnings of the superego, but also with the understanding that her observations of their behaviour were aspects of the workings of the death instinct itself. The harsher and more punitive the superego, the stronger and more destructive the death instinct. The child experiences feelings of pain and anxiety, which are no doubt difficult for the child to endure, and the child may consider that the way out of this pain may be death. The pain may be the result of the needs of the child not being met, so that the child feels uncomfortable, and the tension at times becomes unbearable for the child. The resultant hostile behaviour towards the self is not, for the child, just at the service of destroying himself (i.e. the self-perception of one's own being in the world as the essence of what is wished destroyed). The hostile behaviour is primarily, I think, at the service of destroying the needs and feelings that the child experiences which are causing the unbearable tension.

If the child is hungry and cannot be fed because the parent is unavailable, the child can endure the frustration for a while. Perhaps the fantasy of food satisfies the child for a short period of time, but soon the fantasy is disrupted by the continuance of the pain and the world of the child becomes attacking—essentially, I think, feeling persecuted. No one has come to relieve the pain, and the child, still in pain, interprets this pain as not coming from himself but as coming from an outside source.

> I watched a 2-year-old eating his food; when he tried to take a piece of banana and found that there was none left, he became very angry. He looked at the bowl, and it was as if the bowl had just attacked him. He looked as if he could not believe that there was no more banana, and when his mother offered him another piece, he brushed it aside and off his tray with a sweep of his hand. The child seemed to react as if the banana were bad, because when the mother picked it up and tried to feed it to him, saying, "Here is another piece of banana for you", he simply turned away—but with a fearful expression. I think that he felt that now, not only was the banana bad, but his mother had turned bad and attacking.

Nothing seems good enough for the child at this time, and when the parent tries to feed the child, the child responds to the parent and the food as if they are both destructive and poisonous. Nothing satisfies, and only if parents can "take the feelings into themselves", contain and understand the child's pain and hold them in their minds, will these hostile annihilating phantasies diminish, and the child will once again be able to feed.

The persecutory world is a projected world. The child's hostilities at being in a state of pain cannot be tolerated, and the pain is projected, resulting in the child's world itself becoming hostile and retaliatory. The child's fear of this world and its recoil from it is yet another manifestation of the function of the primitive superego—a superego that is operating from a basis of fear (Alford, 1989). This is, as Alford puts it, "the infant's paranoid fear of attack by what is in reality his own aggression as a manifestation of guilt, albeit an especially primitive one, governed at this stage not by love but by fear" (p. 27). The phantasy is that if the infant could take all the contents of the mother's body, the pain would be gone; but the pain is still present, and, therefore, whatever has been given is not sufficient and more of the contents of mother's body is needed. To need more is to demand more, but to demand more is aggressive, and the resulting anxiety is the fear of retaliation for wanting, needing, demanding more. Persecutory anxiety arises from the death instinct and is the sense of retaliatory phantasies directed against living, destroying a connection between the parent and the ego by destroying a part of oneself—the part that needs the nurturance of the parent.

In the above example of the hungry child, it is the child's internal reactions to the pain and frustration of being hungry that generates the fear and persecutory reactions. It is not the parents per se who are involved in this construction. The perceived goodness or badness of the parents is, to a great extent, the result of the child's internal unconscious phantasies. Even a parent who keeps a child waiting unduly is loved or hated, not simply because they did or did not keep the child waiting, but, rather, because the child has already built up an internal object world that creates a sense of well-being or not well-being, a sense of being or not being. If the unconscious phantasies and the internal world have met up with goodness, which acts to counter the badness, destructiveness, and greed, then the baby can wait for the parent to appear and for a time not feel persecutory anxiety. Of course, the length of time a child must wait for relief is important—we know that some babies can "wait" longer than others, but we also know that some respond to any delay with a sense of persecution. This latter baby has little ego capacity but to perceive immediately that persecution will annihilate, not only what remains of his good internal objects, but also himself.

For the child, the "terror of disintegration and total annihilation is the deepest fear stirred by the operation of the death instinct within" (Abramson, 1986, p. 57). When pain, discomfort, or frustration results in feelings of anger because of nonsatisfying interactions with parents, the anger is threatening to the child. It is experienced as life-attacking, as destroying some part, or all, of the ego. By projecting the hostility outward, a revived persecutory attack is experienced, which is, as Klein points out, the anxiety of one's own hostility perceived as guilt arising out of fear. Thus, the death instinct is not silent, but is given voice by this superego harshness.

The harshness of the superego is also manifested when one thinks that one's pleasures and satisfactions have been gained at the expense of another. The feeling is, then, "I don't deserve to live, I've taken too much from another", and, "They must be angry with me because I haven't left them with enough." Again, a sense of destructiveness arises, aimed at the ego. This is dealt with by becoming unhappy, by becoming unusually giving and/ or helpful, or by destroying oneself or even the other who causes such perceived harm.

The death instinct was present in a depressed 4-year-old whose suicidal behaviour was to try to assuage a severely punitive superego, formed primarily on the basis of internal phantasy (Weininger, 1989).

In an interview, the two distraught parents described how their 4-year-old son continuously questioned them about how bad he was. He asked them to tell him what bad things he had done and how angry they were with him. The parents said that they were hard pressed to describe anything about their son that was either bad or that made them angry. In a loud, crying voice he insisted that they tell him what he did that was wrong and bad. Finally, as the parents told me, they relented and told him that he "dawdled when he went to bed", and that he was "slow" when he was asked to dress himself. With this admission on their part, the child went on to say that they " really couldn't love him", that he was a "bad child", and that maybe they should not "take care of" him any longer. He began to cry inconsolably, and, no matter what the parents did, he cried and said he was a "bad boy".

In another incident, the parents reported that he said that he had "bad thoughts" and began to bang his forehead against the wall. When his mother attempted to cuddle him and stop him from banging his head, he fell out of her arms onto the floor and began, not only to hit his head on the floor, but to pound himself on his body with his fist. This continued for several minutes, and whenever the parents tried to stop this behaviour, the child simply howled and struck himself again. Finally, in exhaustion, he stopped, but he could not be cuddled. He said he was "too bad". He seemed to be saying that he did not deserve being loved, and that he was harbouring some terrible thoughts.

This child also blamed himself when other children, or he, or story-book characters became ill or got hurt. He also blamed himself if something broke, or had a crack in it, or in some way appeared to him less than perfect. On one occasion his father said that he was going to put some air into the tyres of the car, and his son asked, "Did I steal air from the tyres?"

One evening he called for his father or mother to come to his bedroom. When his father appeared, he asked where his mother was, at which point his father said that she was knitting. The boy said, "Why is Mummy knitting? Is it because she hates me?"

At dinner-time the child began a discussion by asking, "Why do very, very old people have to die?" His parents responded, "Many people live a very, very long time. Uncle Sam is very, very old, and he is living. Mummy and Daddy, Granny and Grandad are all going to live for a very long time." The boy asked, "Why, if you get hurt badly, can you die?" The parents replied, "Most of the time peoples' hurts get better, or they take medicine and get better. None of us will have big hurts."

The boy said, "Sometimes when you get angry with me and yell, I worry that I've hurt someone. I worry that you're going to kill me or hurt me. What things do I do that make you angry with me?" He insisted on some examples, and when the parents gave him some, such as "not getting ready for school or not going to bed when asked", he asked for more examples. The parents said that there were only a few examples that made them angry and that "almost all the time you make us feel very happy". The parents also told him, "When we're angry with you, we always love you."

At school, he told his teacher that he did not think anyone liked him. As it was circle time,* she told the children what the boy had said to her. The children called out that they liked him and wanted to play with him. However, the boy sat impassively

---

*A time, usually every day and at the same hour, when the children gather around the teacher to discuss events, to present their ideas, to show an interesting item brought from home, to sing, to recite, and so forth.

and did not appear to be interested in what the children were saying about him. That day he stayed mostly by himself. When another child began to play with him, he asked, "Is there any reason why you don't like me?" While he is no longer fearful of other children, he seems quite unresponsive to their attempts to play with him.

This child's sense of being bad and not deserving affection had been shown for at least two years—since he was about 2—at which time the parents reported that he used to pinch himself, leaving red welts on his skin. They tried to cope with this by putting mitts on his hands to prevent this from occurring. However, he always managed to remove the mitts, either by chewing them or pulling them off, and then he would return to pinching himself.

It does appear that the child's sense of having done something wrong or that something was bad was well developed even by the age of 2. As Klein pointed out, "there could be no doubt that a superego had been in full operation for some time in my small patients of between two and three-quarters and four years of age" (Klein, 1933, p. 248). In this child's case, he phantasized that his badness had hurt or damaged others to the point where they would retaliate and destroy him. He saw himself as having caused others much pain, and not only did he deserve their punishment for his bad deeds or thoughts, but he punished himself by hitting himself. The early projections of his internal object, which he had phantasized as sadistically incorporated by his stealing, robbing, or simply taking, are returning to destroy him.

When I worked with a young boy of 4 years of age, he was able to tell me that he did not "do things right", that he was a bad boy. When I asked him how he thought he was a bad boy, he said, "I have bad things in my head." I paused and said nothing, and he continued, saying that the bad things in his head made him think he was going to do bad things. As we were playing "Hungry Hippo"—a game where a plastic hippo gobbles up and swallows a marble with what might be described as a ferocious leap of jaws—the child said, "I shouldn't grab all the food. I should leave some for Mum and Daddy." I asked him if he thought there was enough food. He answered that he did not know that but added, "I have to make sure there is a lot for my Mummy and Daddy." I interpreted this by saying, "You think there won't be enough for you." He said, "Yes", and continued to have the hippo gobble up the marbles. Then he said the hippo would get a stomach-ache because he had taken too much food and there was none left over. He pointed out that there were no marbles left on the board, and that he had most of them and I had three. I said that I had as much as I needed and that I was glad to see that he could take as much as he needed. I then added, "I think you have a stomach-ache because you took too much food." Again he looked at me and said: "Yes."

Unlike Freud, who said that the superego in young children is silent, I believe it to be very active. In this instance its activity was demonstrated by the intense feelings of self-destructiveness. This child's anxieties are based upon the phantasized sense of anger from the parents for his having taken the food (marbles) and a fear that the real parents are truly angry with him. The fear of the real parents develops because of the distortions in the sense of ego created by the superego. The superego creates the sense in this boy of being bad and that nothing he can do is ever good. In order to relieve himself of the confusion that would be created if he thought he was both good and bad, he perceives himself as only bad. He is a bad boy who must be punished, and now the real parents become the externalized punishers. To retain this sense of badness and not work through the fusion of good and bad results in an ego that sees itself as always bad and remains weak and fragile.

The parents of the child felt that they were good, giving, helpful, and caring parents. They said they neither punished him, nor yelled at him and, in reality, they liked him. They did not think that they had created these "monstrous" feelings of "self-hatred". With considerable feeling and lots of tears they described how they loved him and wanted to know what they could do to make him feel better.

I believe the child's anxieties were related to the object that he had created in his mind—the phantasy object. This object was not totally unlike the real object, the parent, but it was distorted. The extent of this distortion was related to the child's sense of his own hostility towards the real objects. However, it was the internalized parental objects that created for the child the terror of being destroyed, damaged, and attacked.

The superego in this child was, then, a distortion related to the child's strong hostility involved in his desire to take, to devour in an impulsive oral-sadistic way—as the hippo did—his parents' imagined goodness. The child had great difficulty with the resultant thoughts that I suggest might resemble the following: "I want what my parents seem to have. I perceive them as happy as they feed each other and do things for each other. On the other hand, I feel that I am alone and I want the very things that let them do things, enjoy each other, feed each other, talk to each other, even kiss each other. I would like to take these good things for myself. When I do take them, my parents still seem to be kind and good to me. They still seem to love me. I know, however, that I have taken things from them. I think that they will be angry with me when they find out what I have done. Therefore, I must be very angry with me. That will make the thought of what they will do to me when they find out less frightening. Also, my anger at me will stop me from taking any more from them. Indeed, if I can get them to tell me how I am bad, and if I punish myself, they will not hurt me more than I hurt myself." The child has projected his hatred and anger of himself into them, and the parents have become the persecutors. I think that the ego is even further depleted because "the part of the death instinct which is retained in the ego" (Klein, 1958, p. 85), and which can express anger towards the phantasized persecutory parents, only results in even further distress for this child—since the parents are persecutors, to fight them makes them even more persecutory.

Essentially, the child in this depressive position attempts to alleviate the harshness of his superego with his own hurt, he attempts to alleviate the phantasied annihilation that would be meted out to him by his damaged and aggrieved internal parents. The death instinct remains as a source of anxiety about being destroyed from within.

As Federn (1932) suggests, not only is this internal destruction split off from libidinal feelings, but also the libidinal feelings are directed towards the ego not to gratify the ego, but to destroy it (Weiss, 1935). Freud in 1923 (as noted in Rosenfeld, 1990) discusses the "extraordinary intensity of the sense of guilt in melancholia and suggests that the destructive component, a pure culture of the death instinct, has entrenched itself in the superego and turned against the ego. He explains here the fear of death in melancholia by saying that the ego gives itself up and dies because it feels itself hated and persecuted by the superego instead of being loved" (Rosenfeld, 1990, p. 127).

In the above example, the more the real parents said they loved this young boy and did not want him to hurt himself, the stronger his anxieties became—that is, the more severely his superego was expressed. I believe that their goodness was desired, and he wanted what they had, but when they exhibited their goodness, his envy was increased. He did not seem to be able to get what they had that was making them so good to themselves and to each other. He wanted this goodness now in order to curb his sense of badness, yet this desire for their goodness only made him feel guilty, and so he had to continue his self-punishment. In other words, his attacks in phantasy upon the good objects, to rob them and destroy their goodness, resulted in the terror of retaliation. The superego effect of hurting himself was not only to stop his damaging attacks on parents, but to try to eliminate these bad thoughts altogether.

The result of these imagined attacks on parents, as well as the attacks on himself, escalated to the point where his parents were very concerned that he could seriously harm himself, even to the point of killing himself. The child now felt that his parents were very dangerous, and his projected hostility to them was confirmed when they did tell him that he was bad. "In this way each child develops parental images that are peculiar to itself; though in every case they will be of an unreal and terrifying character" (Klein, 1933, p. 251). The phantasy this child had was that the parents wanted him dead because he was bad. In order to try once again to assuage his superego, he did try to kill himself—for example, by running into the street into oncoming traffic. Perhaps in that way he imagined he could kill off the bad parts of himself that were causing such pain to his parents and to himself.

The introjection of a good object was not possible at this time. He saw himself as bad, he felt his parents were always angry with him, he experienced any problems in the home as his fault, and he saw no goodness in himself. He felt he was responsible for all the bad things that happened to anyone. When he felt sad and needed comforting, he felt he did not deserve this comfort and would become angry, particularly when a parent tried to comfort him. The strong sense of destructiveness and annihilation led him to keep away from his parents. The comfort he needed he could not accept, because he felt he was too bad, and, even though his parents did not know it, they represented powerful persecutors. No fusion of good and bad could occur. He felt alone and was being destroyed by himself.

Internal objects

The baby's first object is mother. The baby's first relationship is with its mother. But this is not the whole mother, it is a part-mother or, as Klein suggests, a part-object. It is her nipple, her breast, her eyes, her hair, her hand, her smell, her voice, her smile—it is a part of the mother, and only gradually does the baby become aware that there is actually a whole mother, a whole object who responds to the baby with kindness and containment, or harshness and without containment. This object becomes the first internal object—an aspect of the baby's inner world that is constructed through the interplay of the mechanisms of introjection and projection. These mechanisms start at the beginning of life, and, as Spillius points out, "the inner world is not a replica of the external world; experiences of the external world help to shape the inner world" (Spillius, 1994, p. 328).

At times the parent can accept the demands and cries of the baby; at other times, the demands seem just too much for the parent, and the parent lets the baby "cry it out". After all, so many books have been written suggesting that "it is all right to let the baby cry himself to sleep", or "scream until he realizes he can't get everything his way".

I think that all this does is to provide the baby with a sense that he has little if any internal capacity to cope with the anxiety that exists at the moment. The absence of the parent makes the sense of fear even stronger, and if the parent does not show up, then the baby is sure that the pain, or tension, will never go away. Some babies will fall asleep at this point simply to avoid and deny the continual pain. Then the parent will say, "You see, I knew she would fall asleep."

I think this sleep is an attempt to avoid continual discomfort. The pain may be projected to the parent, leaving the baby's ego weakened, and the sleep itself may be an uncomfortable "fitful" sleep. Due to the baby's inability to cope with the aggression brought on by the pain and the subsequent projection to the parent, the death instinct is brought into sharp focus. The fear of subsequent retaliation by the parent creates a strong sense of having done something very bad and a triggering of the harsh superego, or an attempt to deny bad feelings—a manifestation of withdrawal at the service of survival.

> I met an 11-year-old boy who was unable to fall asleep at night, and, for the two years that he had been bothered by this, he did not, or could not, talk to his parents about this "trouble". Instead, he lay in his bed on his back and worried. His worries were that something terrible was going to happen to his parents—for example, that they would be mugged on the street—and he was afraid that, if he closed his eyes and fell asleep, they would certainly be mugged. I talked to him about his terrible worry, and he said that he thought he would be able to stop the mugging if he stayed awake. By staying awake he could magically keep them safe. With further talk, he said that he wondered whether he could do things in his sleep, "like hurt my parents and not know that I was doing this". I replied that maybe this was why he tried to stay awake. He agreed with a smile and wondered aloud why he was so angry with his parents.

I think his hostility to his parents was very frightening to him, and, by not being able to fall asleep, his anxiety maintained control over his hostilities—yet his hostility created the anxiety of mugging his parents. The harshness of his superego maintained a sense of dread about his anger, yet at the same time denied him understanding of why he worried about them. The anger he experienced towards his parents was unacceptable and was projected to some unknown source that would harm his parents, the muggers. In this way the phantasy of being annihilated by their retaliation was decreased, but at the cost of not being able to fall asleep. The integrity of his ego could then be maintained.

The phantasies associated with the internal object shape the relationships with others in the real world. I think it is essentially the interaction between the person's projections and introjections and the qualities of the real parents that leads to the diminution or the increase in the harshness of the superego. In development, there is usually a gradual buildup of internal objects, and it is within the interaction of this phantasy–real relationship that we mature as we develop our personality, our cognitive abilities, our sensibilities, and a supportive superego.

That children think there are objects that live within their bodies and that these objects have control or exert some influence upon them is illustrated by the following vignettes:

A young mother was taking her 3-year-old daughter for a walk and was leading their dog on a lead. As the three of them walked along quietly, the dog stopped to sniff the ground, and Heather said, "Stop him because there are ants all around." Her mother said that the dog would not eat the ants, but Heather said that he could sniff them in. She added, "He's making so much noise, he's going to sniff in the Mummy ant." She continued, "He'll die if he eats the Mummy ant because the ant will grow spikes when it's inside him and he'll die."

In a similar way a 4-year-old boy had the following conversation with his mother about a sore:

CHILD: Where's the scab on my nose?

MOTHER: It fell off.

CHILD: It's dead, but now it's inside me.

MOTHER: How did it get there?

CHILD: It fell in the hole of my penis, and then I made it go out again.

The scab, an external and visible thing, has dropped off and the child is trying to explain its whereabouts. He perceives it as having gone inside him through his penis but only to be excreted again. The object is real, and the object remains real even if out of sight.

A mother recounts this story about her 3-year-old daughter:

"My 3-year-old came back to me a week after I'd told her that she doesn't have to copy everything her friend says because she has her own special voice inside. She must have mulled over this one. Upon reflection, she said, "You know, Mummy, I don't only have Terry Black inside me. I have a part of you and Daddy inside me too—it's like you're in my pocket all the time so I can keep you safe, but it's really inside me."

This child has incorporated the good combined parents, and to her they are very real. They live in her pocket, yet she is aware that this is just a way of trying to describe a sense that is very difficult to describe, the sense that she knows they are "really inside" her.

Objects are very real for children and for adults as well, except that adults have other ways to describe these internal objects. They use such metaphors as, "I have a lump in my throat" when they are sad or upset, or "I have butterflies in my stomach" when they are frightened, or "It feels like I have rocks in my shoes" when they are so tired they cannot move. We also build up in children a sense of internal objects by such a statement as, "You have the devil in you, that's why you're behaving so badly." Adults tell adults, "You have so much of your father in you, you move just the way he did"; or, "You use the same expressions your mother used when she was your age, you're just like her."

However, when people begin to feel that the good object, which they thought they could count upon, "feels weak" or even begins to turn bad, through the loss of the object, the death of the object, or when they feel that they have been very terrible, difficult, or harsh people, then a sense of doom and fear begins to descend upon them (Weininger, 1992, 1993).

> For example, one 5-year-old boy began to tell me that he had been doing some very bad things, and he did not know why he was doing them. He said it all started when he broke a window in the basement of his house by throwing a ball. He said he was not supposed to throw balls in the house, but he had no one to play with and did not have "anything to do. I was just tossing the ball around and I didn't mean to break the window." He was scolded, told he should not be playing ball in the house, and told to stay outside until he would be allowed back into the house. When he went outside, he said he still did not know what to do and began to dig in the garden. When his father saw him, he told him he was uprooting his bulbs and again scolded the boy. While the child told me that he was crying because everything was going bad, he also recognized he was angry because no one played with him, and he did not know what to do alone. Several more incidents occurred, all of them "bad", and eventually he was told that he was "just bad, and I thought you were such a good boy. Only bad boys would do what you did today."
>
> My discussion with the boy centred around how he "felt inside", and he explained, "I thought that they [parents] liked me, but that was when I was good. Now I can't keep my good anymore—I only have bad. It's too much for me, and I don't know what to do." I asked him why he could not keep things good inside himself any more. His response was, "I finished all the maple syrup this morning, and my Mum said only a selfish kid would do that." Obviously, he felt that he was selfish and that he was taking food that should be shared. Now the food would "go bad" in him, and this spoiling would cause his internal goodness to become bad, and then he would do more bad things—as he told me he had done—and could not stop himself now. I asked if there was any way I could help him so that his goodness would be stronger. He said, "Yeah, take out the maple syrup and give it back." I said we could not do that, but perhaps we could do something else. He replied, "I don't think so. I think I'm so bad I won't

live." He felt that his internal objects had become so bad that they could not be made to feel better, and perhaps he was not worthwhile. His anger became directed towards himself.

I suggested that we go for a walk, and as we were walking, I said that I knew a bakery where we could buy some sweet rolls. He said he was not hungry, so I pointed out that we did not have to eat them right now, we could take them home. As we neared the shop, I told him that he would choose the sweet rolls, any kind and as many as he thought he needed. Inside the shop he selected several varieties, all of which had sugar water dripped on them, were covered with chocolate, and had white cream oozing out somewhere in the roll. He told me that we needed 20 rolls. We bought 20 rolls, and I gave them to him to carry home, and he did so with a smile. He did not eat any on the way home, and once home we placed all 20 on a large plate and took them to the family members, offering everyone as many as they wished. Of course, everyone took at least one, and, as each left the plate, the child's happiness increased, so that when only three were left, he was delighted. At this point, I asked him how his insides felt, and he whispered in my ear, "My insides are really good now." He had not eaten a single sweet roll.

A sense of deteriorating goodness combined with a sense of being overpowered by badness reinforced his view that his parents "knew" he was bad. This overwhelmed this young boy and made him feel as if he would die because badness was becoming so strong. A sense of depressive anxiety was prominent, and the child had no way of working this through by himself. Our friendship and his trust in me to contain his anxieties, along with our capacity to restore the "good" feeling he needed to feel from his parents, enabled him to regain his usual sense of happiness and desire to live. The combined effect of demonstrating to his family that he had some good things to give them to eat, along with the family taking and eating these good things and remaining healthy, reassured the boy that his internal objects were not so bad as to destroy his family. His harsh superego became "easier" as his anticipated fear that his objects would only harm others did not materialize. External reality distilled his phantasy by not validating it again.

When the child has internalized a good object, he can express his feelings without anxiety of retaliation or death. However, where the baby has been unable to introject good objects, or where consistent good objects are unavailable for the first few years of life, then the baby will not be able to experience adequate interactions between introjections and projections. As a result, the child's ego capacity to cope with a sense of annihilation resulting from frustrating objects or even abuse will be very poor. The child will not be able to "attach" to parents. This lack of attachment unfortunately further prevents the introjection of good objects. Lack of attachment also creates an inner world that responds to interactions involving internal or external frustration with suspicion, fear of manipulation, and an overriding sense of being annihilated. The death instinct, the child's "fear of real objects—its phobic anxiety—is based upon its fear of its unrealistic superego and of objects which are real in themselves, but which it views in a phantastic light under the influence of its superego" (Klein, 1933, p. 249). The death instinct cannot be overcome if there are no good and effective containing experiences with parents or caregivers. There are no "islands" within the ego to cope with the sense of annihilation resulting from projections of frustration, even mild frustration, and subsequent retaliation.

The attacks by this child directed at his caregiver or environment then become the child's attempts either to ward off the annihilation or, as one child said, "to not make it worse". That is, this sense in the child of becoming overwhelmed by external or internal impulses, either real or imagined, will result in the expression of hostility. This hostility is not intended to destroy the child but rather to destroy the source of the perceived or phantasized frustration. There are no other ways for such a child to cope. All the child can do is to destroy the world around him, even though within this destruction is the child's own destruction. There is no capacity to depend upon, to rely upon. or to be contained by caregivers. Trust is not established. There is no object within the ego to "resonate" with a sense of goodness that came from someone else. Goodness from the caregiver would have resulted in some sense of internal goodness, an introjected good object. In this child there is either no good object, or it is not strong enough to grapple with all the bad objects that continue to feel so persecutory. This child has only bad experiences of rejection and abuse, of neglect and aggression directed at him by non-giving caretakers. The result is that frustration is experienced so often that the ego cannot cope with the accompanying sense of internal inadequacy. This continual frustration is felt as an ego threat to continued being. Therefore, the child accuses others, hits out, becomes angry, and destroys all that seems to be a threat to the fragile ego.

The child's destruction of the environment is an attempt to stop the sense of ego annihilation, even though the destruction of any nurturing dependency and love from the caregivers will also result in the further annihilation of the ego. In this way, death comes to this child, either through the destruction of the child's being and environment and/or through isolation and total protective independence. The ego's destruction, yet imagined as safety, is then accomplished. Some children I have known have expressed this as they told me such things as, "This is the way out" . . . "Maybe Jesus will be a better guy" . . . "Maybe I'll be born again" . . . "I can't stop myself—I just gotta be bad but drugs make me feel safe" . . . "I'll kill anyone who tries to get close to me, they all hurt you." These children are 6 to 12 years of age, and their chances of "making it" lessen with each month of their isolating and isolated lives.

> One young boy of 2 years would try to poke his finger in his adopted mother's eye whenever she held him. He was adopted at 1 year of age, and the little information the adoptive parents were given was that he was a neglected infant who had sometimes been starved. He was removed from his biological parents and offered for adoption at 10 months of age. The adoptive mother tried to feed him, but he spit the food at her. She tried to tuck him into bed, but he would urinate on her as she came close to him. It seemed as if there was nothing she could do to get close to her son—he always rejected her. He would not let his father come close to him either, but he did not try to poke his eyes out. His parents put food in a plate, and he would take it as long as they did not look at him. The parents reported that he was very active, "hyper", and "always bumping into things and breaking anything he could get hold of". The parents tried to get help, and

they maintained the visits and the support and help they received, but the child did not seem to get better, nor allow them to get close to him. He could not internalize any goodness, and, if he even had bits of goodness "instilled", he quickly seemed to destroy them or the goodness became overwhelmed by his sense of internal badness. For example, his mother gave him a sweet, and at first he sucked vigorously on the sweet and "seemed to smile", but soon he spat it out vigorously. Also, there were times his parents did kiss him lightly, and he scrubbed at that part of his body that was kissed as if to wash off the kisses.

The parents felt they could do nothing for the child. He did not respond to their loving care, and he was not responsive to treatment, medical or psychological. He seemed to be a "lost child"—and perhaps he was. He seemed unable to internalize anything good and was always on guard, as if expecting everything to be bad and to be hurt by everyone. Eventually, within three years, the adoption broke down, and the child was placed in a psychiatric setting.

I have observed that some young children, when they eat, stuff food into their mouths. I often hear the parent say, "Finish that mouthful first, then take some more", sometimes preventing the child from filling its mouth to overflowing. Some children will stop eating if their parents prevent them from mixing the foods on the plate or from stuffing the food into their mouths, and they resume eating only when they can "stuff the food in". Some children want to feel their food as they eat, and they chew in the "front of their mouth" with their front teeth; they seem to gain a lot of pleasure from having these oral "fill-ups". Then there are many children and also adults who "save the best piece for the last". They select the "very best morsel" and relish the thought that they still have that special piece of food to eat, as if the meal and the goodness of the meal will continue on, perhaps forever.

Margaret Fries (1935) talked about the eating experience when she wrote that "infants want to crowd the experience of food intake with the experience of warmth and affection from mother" (p. 234). Perhaps the taking in of food is the taking in of mother, and the stuffing in of food is the acquisition of lots of good internal objects all at once, or as much as you can get at one time! The crowding of food in the mouth, the crowding of good feelings from mother, the saving the best for the last and making sure the good object will always be there is, I think, an attempt to manage feelings and emotions. Sperling (1948) discusses this and says it is:

> . . . normally a basic function of the psychic apparatus, representing Freud's dualism of basic drives. The psychic apparatus, in the service of the death instinct, works in the direction of mastering and eliminating stimuli from within and without, in this way keeping psychic tension at the lowest possible ebb. Such dividing and spacing can easily be recognized as a mechanism of the death instinct. In the crowding of emotions there appears to be a manifestation of eros (life instinct). [pp. 234–235]

If we place the food in a bowl in front of the child, allow the child to eat as the child wishes, compliment the child on "taking good food into the tummy", and are not concerned as to whether the food is "stuffed in the mouth" or mixed together with other foods, the child seems to eat "better" and with fewer "feeding problems". I am aware that the child needs to eat a certain amount at each meal, but I think that, with parent encouragement and compliments, the child will eat his stuffed-in meal and perceive it as getting good objects given by the loving and accepting parents.

To object to the messy eating habits of young children is to ask for trouble. These children will then perceive food as given, not to support and encourage their good internal objects, but, rather, as something "controlling" and "bad". Often they will refuse to eat. I think they fear that the external controlling parents, who are felt as "bad" by the child, will, in fact, make the bit of food they have inside their other internal objects turn bad and render them less able to cope with their sense of anger and the death instinct.

Phantasied and real people, the internal objects and external parents, shape our relationships with people in our outer world. Our interactions with projections and introjections of our children are complex, and through our responses to their feelings—those expressed by the children and those felt by us—we structure their developing personality organization. This is a relational model, and responses are always contextually based. We respond to children not simply on the basis of what we feel, but also on the basis of the feelings that children project into us. We respond in a countertransferential manner, and we must be able to think about our reactions before we simply respond to our children. We must be able to decontaminate or, as Bion (1967) has said, detoxify these projections. Then we can give them back to the child, not as we received them, but with part of our thoughts and feelings added; that is, our internal resources become the food for their effective personality organization. The children then introject good objects (Weininger, 1992, 1993).

CHAPTER FOUR

The paradoxical compromise
of not being: early oral sadism
and incorporation of a cruel
superego that is both protective
and destructive of the ego

Sarah, age 40, has been in treatment for four years now, and only recently has she been able to talk about her early childhood. She says that she remembers nothing before she was a teenager and, even then, most of her memories and thoughts are events that happened outside her home. She has begun to talk about how hard it is for her to feel anger. The following are excerpts from her therapy.

> Sarah thinks that anything that stirs up anger for her is "not recorded" and has to be camouflaged. "The camouflage makes me feel safe; anger is not a safe thing for me to feel." She adds, "I always feel unsafe—a pervasive thing, not at any particular time. I know that if I get angry, something terrible will happen, and something terrible happened—an all-pervasive sense of not being safe."
>
> "I was safe as long as the attention was given to others and I could be someone who always did the right thing, like succeed in school. However, even then it wasn't my success that was seen; it was that my siblings were pointed out as being

less than adequate because here I was, a girl who did well, and they, my brothers, were supposed to do better than me.

"I watched everything. I was always on the outside. I never felt like I was taken into account. I was sure that if I was taken into account, they (my family) would hurt me. No one but my father was ever taken into account. And no one else's needs were ever taken into account. No one was ever allowed to feel satisfied except my father and maybe, to a lesser degree, my mother.

"I always felt that children didn't exist as individuals in their own right; they just existed as some adjunct at the level of flowers—do well, water it, give it plant food, show it off. I was given the physical necessities, but children were like plants. You see them, they're supposed to be beautiful, but they don't talk, and they don't do anything. They just exist because father gave them food and water.

"And girls were difficult because father did not like girls. I had to camouflage myself to live. I had to not look nice and not really want anything, because that would make me real and a person and I'd be in some great danger, I thought.

"I never thought I'd live this long—I thought I'd be dead when I was a child, and here I'm 40 years old. I can't remember not having this as a fundamental assumption and that I wouldn't live as long as my parents. I can't remember when I didn't think that others in my family thought of running away from home for some reason, probably to be safe, but not me. I just stuck it out where I was. I didn't have a number—an age when I'd die. I knew that I would just not live long as an adult.

"Adults counted, and I did not count. I couldn't count. Adults are independent and successful, I couldn't be. I could not think of what I would be as a grown-up because it was not possible for me to grow up. I never grew up. If I did, then I would count, and then my father would be very angry with me. I would be a real person.

"So I went to school with no special goals. I thought this out very logically—no goals, just go to school. I found logic to be my safety—laws would not be questioned, and laws would make me safe. The main law is that I would die soon, and if I counted I'd die sooner."

I said that success that made her a real person did not seem possible. Questioning things would not be possible. She said, "Questioning was not part of me. I could be successful at school because this never related to my sense of life success. The two are divorced. I could never consider life success, and my father would never consider that a girl could be successful.

"I made laws to protect me. I couldn't even be a pretty flower. It was too dangerous to be pretty and clever. To even have something pretty was dangerous. My laws and logic saved me. I grew very fat, but I was still clever. I felt I could be safe and wait for my inevitable death.

"My mother didn't count either. She didn't or couldn't protect us—no one ever questioned anything my father did. He was so cruel to people. He never admits anything—it's never his fault. Everything that happens that he doesn't like is caused by someone else. He doesn't recognize that he is such a terrible man."

I suggested to her that to do something that made her think that she had done something, like living and counting as a person, would make him very angry. She replied, "Yes he'd probably strike you dead—he'd kill his child—but I thought I would be responsible for my death—I'd make him kill me."

Aggressiveness, in the form of destruction and annihilation, remained in this woman as an internal object, an object that developed as a result of the real parent perception and the phantasy perception. The interaction created an internal object that allowed her to live as long as she did not count as a person. She must never do anything that would threaten the phantasy and reality of her perceived father as someone who would destroy her if she succeeded in being more than a stationary beautiful flower—one that would eventually die, as all flowers do sooner or later. Her success, then, in simply living, was t o recognize that she would die. However, to do this, she saw herself as someone who had to make up laws to survive—laws that made her life limited, narrow, and devoid of strong feelings of love and hate. She perceived these emotions as dangerous because having them meant that you counted as a person, and that meant imminent death. The laws allowed her to live for a while longer but, as she thought, never into adulthood. The life instinct that fuses with the death instinct could never be stronger than the death instinct, for that in itself meant death!

If the need to succeed, to be a person, and to be an adult woman became strong, then dying was felt to be the consequence. At the same time, the need to destroy that need most certainly meant death. This was a paradoxical and extremely conflictual situation.

The conflict presented itself clinically by her excessive weight gains, by her never taking herself into account, and by her always being available to others to do whatever they asked of her. In effect, she was their messenger, driver, and servant and was rarely offered anything for her help. Sarah neither asked for anything from others, nor did she expect anything. While she was often hurt and misused by others, she either never complained or seemed not to be able to recognize what happened to her. She simply went on "not counting" and being safe—making new laws to control all aspects of her behaviour so that she would never count. When she might begin to think that she was counting as a person, she put an end to it with a law that stated, "You must do everything possible to make sure you take no credit for the work. Pass the credit on to someone else." She managed at work to have supervisors who made her think her work was inadequate even if she knew that that was not true. She had a law that said, "You can't do anything about that. Just realize once again you don't count and will never count. If you count, you die."

The sorrow she experienced by not counting was partially offset by the sense that she was safe for a while. Her self-destructiveness was never perceived as that—rather, she experienced the narrowing of her life as a way of saving herself. She gained some satisfaction in seeing herself as "plain and not counting" and created another law—"to be plain and not count meant you had outsmarted father—but then to outsmart father meant you counted." This law meant her certain death. Her response to this was to turn away from any situation that could lead to anxiety. She went to work, she spoke to people at work, but when she went home she did very little except prepare a simple meal and feed herself.

Her hostility towards her father was so violent and all-pervasive in her life that the primary function of her harsh superego was to force the ego to develop mechanisms by which it could fend off these violent thoughts. Her ego was continually in danger of being overwhelmed by her death if she counted. To count meant the destruction of a hated father, and her death. The superego acted to prevent this act by not allowing the ego to count, to feel important, or to matter.

Her sadism—her hostility towards father—could not be satisfied. She could only cook her meals at night and eat alone, expressing an oral sadistic phantasy of cannibalistically eating the hated father. This led to her feeling guilty, although she did not understand why she felt so bad. She tried to eat more and more to counteract the sense of badness that the food gave her. The severity of her superego was gradually diminished as she felt the pains of eating too much. Perhaps these pains were sufficient to satisfy the superego (relieving the cause of her sense of guilt brought about by her then unconscious hostility towards her father), as well as giving her a sense of desire to continue to live. In this way her ego, for the moment, is freed from the excess sadistic tension, experienced as anxiety. The harshness and control of the superego, derived from the death instinct, becomes less severe as the pain is experienced as an ego function over which she has some control. The very real power of her father to withhold satisfactions, gratifications, and pleasure from her initiated in her a sense of impending death, because she desired such satisfaction, not only from her real father but from her superego. The orally incorporated object became the feared object and thereby created a "fear of [her] own sadistic impulses" (Klein, 1933, p. 251). She feared the phantasied attacks the object would make on her, which, she felt, would destroy her. Klein states: "the formation of the super-ego begins at the same time as the child makes its earliest oral introjection of its objects . . . the small child becomes dominated by the fear of suffering unimaginable cruel attacks, both from its real objects and from its super-ego" (Klein, 1933, p. 251).

The anxiety that Sarah would experience would be interpreted by her as her desire to destroy the hostile objects—
internally and in reality—and this would only increase her sense
of anxiety. If she imagined that she could destroy the real father,
her anxiety mounted. Her superego became harsh and severe
and only reminded her that, if she destroyed him, then she
counted, and she would die. Thus, she could not count and she
suffered; her world became lonely as, being lonely, she realized
she did not count. With this realization her anxiety lessened,
and the phantasied onslaught and the subsequent revenge was
curbed. Loneliness and eating both provided pain and also over-
came for a time the sense of counting and the fear of dying. Her
laws protected her but made her life very narrow and circum-
scribed.

Another patient of mine for five years, a woman of 55 years,
described the following short dream, which, along with subsequent associations, points to the death instinct as a "clinically
loud" manifestation.

> "I went to the window in the middle of the night. I was sure
> there were some people out there ready to get me." She went
> on to say, "I awakened in a sort of panic and I had to go to the
> window to look out. No one was there."

I asked her to continue after she paused for a few minutes:

"I had been to a party the night before, and there were so
many important people there who had such big ideas. When
they were dancing, I thought how ridiculous this looks, and
they don't know it. I thought that they shouldn't be exhibiting
themselves like that. It didn't seem right because they were
so important.

"My partner was feeling pleased with himself and wanted to
dance. I didn't want to, although ordinarily I do, but this time
I now know that I didn't want to because I would be seen as
ridiculous, because I was dancing too much, and too many
people would be looking at me. So I went very reluctantly to
dances, but I didn't dance much."

I asked her if she would talk about a word she used a few
times—"ridiculous". She said, "I would be 'puffed up' because I would be enjoying myself, and when I enjoy myself,

then someone pays for this—me. I know the other people would say that I am not bright enough to enjoy myself. I don't have important ideas. So I didn't really want to dance. I'd be ridiculous, and they would be looking at me too much. They would know I didn't have the right to dance.

"I thought, 'They have what I want—they're in control, they know so much, they're in charge of themselves and can let themselves go. I can't.' I'm jealous of what they have. Then I expect that they would be very angry with me if they knew that I was jealous of them. They would know this if I danced too much, because they would see me as 'puffed up' and hate me. If I'm 'puffed up', then someone pays for that. My mother told me as a child that Jesus died because of `puffed up' people.

"I know my father died because of me. I blame myself because I should have been with him when he needed me before he died, and I was too busy studying at University. I'm paying for his death. I'll pay until I die. The price of my being happy is death, because, if I'm happy, then I pay for it. I'll die. I should have helped him and not pleased myself. I 'puffed myself up' by going to University. I thought I could learn, but that only meant I'm 'puffed up', and then there would be a big price to pay. I'd be smart and maybe even a good person, but then I know I'd eventually lose everything. I can't be all right."

To be pleased and happy suggests to my patient that object relationships have improved and that there is some sense of development, not only in a social sense, but also in an intellectual sense. At such times she would be able to perceive her partner as loving her and as being pleased to be with her—but then she would quickly begin to suspect that, if her partner got too close to her, he would actually know how bad she was. For example, he would know that she was a jealous person, one who did not think she did the right things, and one who tried to puff herself up and always at some expense to others—in particular to her father. She is sure that by not being at home and by being at University (away from her home) she was "puffing herself up", and the cost was her father's life. Learning and closeness to others has always been very difficult for her. She thinks of herself as dumb, if not stupid—someone who cannot seem to do the right thing or say the right things. She would rather be by herself, because she is "inept". Women who meet her seem to be friendly towards her and they telephone her, but she does not telephone them. She telephones them when she thinks she is too dumb to find the answer by herself. When they help her with the answer, she then thinks, "they know how dumb I am, they wouldn't want me to be with them. They wouldn't want me as a friend."

This woman has incorporated a very harsh image of her parents—her mother in particular. Her image of her mother is that she is never pleased with her or with what she does. Yet, in reality, her mother has told her how pleased she is with her education and with her present work. However, as soon as my patient allows herself to think that her mother is pleased with her, she feels "puffed up" and remembers that Jesus died for this reason. Her father died for this reason as well. So she is not able to accept her mother's sense of her. Instead, she accepts her own harsh view of herself as dumb and "inept". The phantasy is more potent and powerful than the reality.

Her introjected harsh objects are continually projected to reality, and she responds to reality as attacking and unsatisfying. She talks about her early life with her father as a time when she always tried to please him and make him happy, and whenever she did succeed she always experienced her mother as being angry with her. She accepted this as a punishment for making her father happy, as this was someone that her mother "rightfully" should have made happy. She felt guilty, yet she could not prevent herself from making him laugh and, as she said, "be happy". The anticipated anger and retaliation from her mother for doing this was enacted by running out into traffic or climbing onto porch railings and trying to walk on them as on a tightrope. She usually fell off the railing but was never struck by a car when she ran into oncoming traffic. However, when she was hurt, her mother would tell her, "You go to your father—you're his—not mine." Then the whole cycle was repeated—she would go to him, he would give her some comfort, she would make him happy, and then she would feel guilty and try to hurt herself once again.

In this patient, the sense of a cruel superego was related to the intensity of her aggression towards both her mother and father—her mother for not comforting her, and her father for not understanding why she felt she had to make him happy. That is, she felt that since her mother was not making her father happy, she had to do this, even though her mother would be angry. She consciously anticipated that her mother would be pleased because she was helping her. In this situation, as well as in the previous examples, the oedipal conflict is obviously strong—but here I am describing aspects of the oral–sadistic incorporation, the subsequent strength of the superego, and the retaliation from external objects, all of which are unconsciously felt as annihilation and as bringing about the death of the ego (Weininger, 1992, 1993).

"Counting" for my first patient or being "puffed up" for my second patient seem to mean the same thing and represent being important. In both clinical examples this resulted in a sense of being, or becoming, annihilated. In both cases, the superego is very strong. Thus, "to count" or to be "puffed up" is not tolerable, because this is understood by both patients as that their own desires will be satisfied, *but* at the expense of the death of another. To achieve success is perceived as having destroyed, or at least damaged, the parent. The result of this hostility will be the threat of annihilation, from the harsh superego, from the parents, and subsequently from others whom these patients put in a position to be harmful. It is as if to be a person and to be someone is to stand out—to show what one knows and what one can do. However, this is very dangerous to do, because this makes one sufficiently conspicuous in that standing out or showing what one knows so that what is done is seen as an expression of some form of aggression. This is intolerable, because the consequence of aggression is death.

In a way, then, the superego is protective—it does not let one stand out, it keeps one so anxious that one cannot do anything to stand out—one cannot learn, one cannot study, one cannot behave in any "free way", because the person would be seen as "ridiculous"—one would stand out! However, this superego, as a manifestation of the death instinct, is harsh, cruel, and limiting. Its strength is derived from the oral–sadistic introjection of phantasized parents, with subsequent phantasized revenge from these objects, which threaten annihilation of the ego. The clinically loud voice of the death instinct is heard in superego demands that, in themselves, threaten death *unless* certain events occur. In the last two examples those events meant not to count and not to matter as a person. By not counting, the superego will not seek revenge, because, "I am not important enough to be killed", and the death instinct is assuaged, for a time at least.

In this way the superego becomes a protector yet a destroyer of the ego—a protector in that the warnings are, "Do something to appease the revengeful objects", and a "destroyer" by annihilating the ego potentials. Clinically these features seem to be important in sorting through the early oral sadistic introjections and the manner in which the superego developments occur. This early superego is seen as partly protective and partly destructive. Its manifestations in interactions with real events and experiences with parents limit both emotional and cognitive development (Weininger, 1993).

CHAPTER FIVE

The beleaguered ego: defences against the death instinct

The ego, in order to survive the threats of annihilation by the death instinct, projects these threats outwardly and, in this way, tries to win the struggle between the life and death instincts. The death instinct is, as well, made into aggressive impulses (Klein, 1957b).

> The ego splits itself and projects that part of itself which contains the death instinct outward into the original object—the breast. Thus the breast, which is felt to contain a great part of the infant's death instinct, is felt to be bad and threatening to the ego, giving rise to a feeling of persecution. In that way, the original fear of the death instinct is changed into fear of a persecutor. . . . Part of the death instinct remaining in the self is converted into aggression and directed against the persecutors. [Segal, 1973, p. 25]

> The ego is constantly protecting itself against the pain and tension to which anxiety gives rise, and therefore makes use of defences from the beginning of post-natal life. . . . If its capacity to cope with anxiety is inadequate, the ego may return regressively to earlier defences, or even be driven to

the excessive use of those appropriate to its stage. As a result, persecutory anxiety and the methods of dealing with it can be so strong that subsequently the working-through of the depressive position is impaired. [Klein, 1957b, p. 61]

Anxiety creates the need for ego defences, especially the mechanism of splitting, particularly when strong persecutory anxiety is experienced. The working through of this persecutory anxiety in the treatment process is significantly restricted when the "patient clings to a strong positive transference" (Klein, 1957b, p. 73). I think difficulty is primarily organized around idealization as a defence in order to split off hate and envy of the therapist.

When the ego is confronted by strong destructive impulses, which Klein believes to be "the expression of the death instinct",

. . . the patient feels exposed to destruction while he is in the process of accepting these impulses as aspects of himself and integrating them. That is to say, the patient at certain times faces several great dangers as a result of integration: his ego may be overwhelmed; the ideal part of his self may be lost when the existence of the split-off destructive and hated part of the personality is recognized; the analyst may become hostile and retaliate for the patient's destructive impulses which are no longer repressed, thus also becoming a danger- ous super-ego figure; the analyst, insofar as he stands for a good object, is threatened with destruction. [Klein, 1957b, p. 73]

The following vignette illustrates the way in which one indi- vidual responded to the feeling of becoming exposed to this sense of destruction and annihilation.

My patient, a man of 44 years, has been in treatment for two years now and has felt some significant improvements, in that he has been able to work, has become aware of his destructive relationships, and is in the process of understanding his rage at his parents for their serious neglect and abuse of him as a young child.

However, in trying to meet the ego dangers arising as a result of treatment, including the hate and envy towards the therapist, but at the same time trying to maintain the sense of an ideal therapist, my patient felt he had to maintain a sense of being in control of his anger. However, it was becoming more and more difficult for him to do so. The danger, as he said, was that the therapist might respond to his anger and retaliate. If this were to happen, the patient would feel as if he were losing the ideal part of his self. The clinical danger in this case was that if he did not recognize and understand his anger, then treatment would end prematurely. He would feel that he was in charge and in control and that he had nothing more to gain from being in treatment.

My patient reported the following dream:

"I had moved into a warehouse that had space on three levels. The entrance level was at the ground level and contained mostly living space, while the sleeping level was on another level. Two men shared the place with me. I didn't know them. Then a black-haired woman with a blonde woman came to the entrance and wanted to have sex. I knew this would disturb my other two roommates. I was asleep when they arrived at the door and I got up, puttered around groggily, washed my face, and looked for condoms, but I seemed to be avoiding something. I went back to bed, and the blonde woman disappeared to find the other guys. When I was in bed, the black-haired woman was in bed beside me. I did not do anything. I lay still, thinking, "it's up to her." At first I was ill at ease, as if there was an expectation for me to perform. She made no move, and I fell asleep and felt relieved to fall asleep, content that nothing had happened."

After describing the dream, he began to talk about the dream, saying:

"I don't know who the women are. You have to be there somewhere. You invade me. I hate you more because you help me and because I hate the helper. One part of me is beyond help—no one can help that part of me succeed, and I will only put on window dressing to look as if I'm o.k. There is no complete way to help me to feel better. I will prove my strength and help my helplessness survive. I feel enraged by the helpless part of me being helped, and I'm fighting to remain helpless. Part of me is willing to be helped and tries to take over, but by being helpless, I am enraged and I remain helpless. I think I must be destroying the helper; I want to destroy everything and everyone, and this makes me become even more desperate because then I know I must be losing some ground and getting help. I want to have help, but I don't want you to help me. I want help, but I don't want help. I really feel weak if I think you can help me. I am supposed to be very strong.

"Maybe the black-haired woman is part of me, a projection of the me who wants to be helpless and unattractive and who seduces me at the same time, just by being present, by waiting for me to let myself be lowered to the lowest and showing nothing seductive except my own weakness, and that would show the weakness of my helpable part. The part that would be shown and I would know would be the unhelpable part, because it yielded to the helpless, and the helpless would win. It would be a moral victory. I deserve to not be helped because I am weak.

"The black-haired woman has these full breasts. She is a stupid woman. All she has are breasts, and since she is stupid her breasts are stupid. She has nothing to give. I lay there realizing that there is nothing there that I want or maybe nothing I can get and maybe it isn't going to be all right to take anything because it is stupid. Maybe it's the part of me that is stupid."

This patient's ego is confronted by very strong destructive feelings, and I think they are experienced as being sufficiently strong to kill him. However, as treatment is progressing, his ego is in the process of recognizing and beginning to accept the bits of anger as his. His attempts to introject these aggressive bits of himself are so threatening that he is sure that he will not survive. The part of his ego that he identifies as being held safe for him by me is at times seen as idealized, yet at times weak, because it needs to be kept safe by someone else other than himself. Since I am holding part of him, then at times I must become the bad one—that is, since I am containing his weak part, I must also be weak, and, if I am weak, I would not be able to survive the anger that he is beginning to experience. He laughs about his anger and says, "Sometimes I feel very angry at you. I don't know why. Maybe it is because I've let you get too close to me. No, maybe because I've become too close to you and you know how bad I really am." I interpret his sense of badness as his concern that he will destroy me, at first by trying to minimize my help and then by killing himself. As he experiences his attempts to minimize my help and the relationship, he is sure that it is I who will become very angry with him and then, as he said, "You'll just toss me out of here like a dog. You don't care what happens to me. I know you can't let me become angry. I know you'll be afraid and want me to leave." In this way I think he sees that the destructive part is projected to me and is afraid I would retaliate. The strength of his projected sadism determines the strength of my imagined retaliation. I have become his harsh superego.

His sense of annihilation is very strong. My patient does not know whether he will be able to hold onto his own anger and, if he does not, the therapist will become an even stronger persecutory figure. My patient's annihilation would then be his phantasied outcome. He must either defend himself by further projection, carrying with it the fear of continued persecution and retaliation, which will quickly lead to the dissolution of treatment, or he must abruptly quit treatment. I think the strong anxiety (because of premature attempts to undo the splitting) must be interpreted—that the breast, the primal object, the source for him of anticipated goodness, is not destroyed and is available. That the breast is not stupid and his desire for the breast as a good introjected object is not stupid, that he is not stupid for feeling that he needs this comfort and nurturance. His attempts to minimalize treatment are his attempts to behave in a superior way because he thinks his therapist will hate him for being such a "difficult person" (the patient's words) and for trying to minimize the therapist's contribution to the treatment process. The therapist is "stupid", the therapist is the stupid breast, and to take from the breast is to prove how stupid you are.

When I interpreted this, his response was, "I had to keep her goodness in the dark. This let me feel I could do everything on my own. You wouldn't be angry with me because I wouldn't take too much from you, just a bit, and then I wouldn't even have to feel weak. Maybe I could fool myself."

When he is faced with the reality of being dependent on the analyst, standing for the parent, particularly the mother, he would prefer to die, to be non-existent, to deny the fact of his birth and also to destroy his analytic progress and insight representing the child himself, which he feels the analyst, representing the parent, has created. . . . It appears that these patients have dealt with the struggle between their destructive and libidinal impulses by trying to get rid of their concern and love for their object by killing their loving dependent self and identifying themselves almost entirely with the destructive narcissistic part of the self which provides them with a sense of superiority and self-admiration. [Rosenfeld, 1971, p. 174]

Rosenfeld went on to explain:

. . . contact with help is experienced as weakening the patients' narcissistic omnipotent superiority and exposing him to conscious feelings of overwhelming envy which were strictly avoided by his previous detachment. [Rosenfeld, 1990, p. 110]

CHAPTER SIX

Transference/countertransference issues in a patient "addicted" to death

A 35-year-old male patient of mine seems driven to kill himself. He has been attempting to prove to himself that he is immune to AIDS, that no matter how many male partners he has and no matter what kind of unprotected sex he involves himself in, he will not develop AIDS. He has been trying to prove this for about fifteen years, and so far he has not contracted AIDS. We have been working together for three years.

This man has a history of physical and sexual abuse since infancy and experienced this abuse from both his mother and father. When he first came into treatment, he talked "freely" about how his father wanted to watch him while he took a bath when he was a young boy of about 7 or 8 years, and how he would inspect his anus with a flashlight in order to make sure that he did not have "worms". Later he began to remember that his father would have him play "horsey" with him, nude upon the father's nude body, and the boy always had to slide off the father's rear and make contact with his father's anus with his penis. His father would attempt to have anal sex with his son on many occasions, usually at night, or would come to lie "close" in bed with him. This sexual abuse continued for years, with the son unable to think of a way that he could escape this abuse. His mother would beat him with brooms, sticks, or anything she could "lay her hands on", and he came home from school expecting to be beaten by his mother. He would try to enter the house silently and hide in a closet while his mother ran around the house screaming and banging a stick on the walls, doors, and furniture looking for him. He would hide from her in the basement, yet she often beat him with sticks. However, in the basement he would see his father going through erotic magazines. He remembers thinking as a child that his father just seemed to be waiting for him.

Throughout this physical and sexual abuse, he went to school, excelled at school, and became very popular, particularly with the girls, who, he says, often tried to seduce him. Although, he rarely dated girls, he did seduce a number of his male classmates to have sex with him.

In later adolescence he turned to religion, determined to stop his homosexual behaviour by praying to God and by offering himself to his church. He became a minister, but, while given recognition by his congregation for his religious knowledge and zeal, he could not stop his homosexual encounters, which, he said, numbered into the hundreds on single weekends.

He did marry and had children, but he described his sexual activity with his wife as "work"—she wanted him to be aggressive with her in their sexual acts and often hurt him by insisting that he "use" his penis in ways that made it very painful for him. He continued with his marriage and with his homosexual behaviour. When he realized that his God and religion were not helping him at all, he left the pulpit. His wife left him, and he said that he felt "like a man wandering through the desert with no one to turn to except all those gay guys who seemed to want me." His homosexual behaviour increased considerably, and he continued to "flirt with aids", as if death was now a goal. However, by living and remaining physically well, he felt there was a vestige of his religion saying to him that his God was continuing to protect him from AIDS even though he was not changing his sexual behaviour.

He started into treatment almost as a "joke", as if a "mere mortal" was going to help him when God could or did not, and he said that he thought of himself as a devil who was at war with

God. Perhaps with me he would have his fight "on earth rather than in heaven" and could battle me for his death.

Death to him would be desirable and even helpful to mankind, because he "wouldn't infect anyone any more" and he "wouldn't seduce anyone" in "mind" or in "body". He was insistent that he should die, that he would be pleased to die, and that, while he would work with me to help himself, he would also fight me with "everything that he had".

The "everything" turned out to be his attempt to create in me an exceptional feeling and sense of sadness and despair, a sense in me that whenever he told me of his terrible early childhood and of the extreme difficulties he was having now, I would succumb by feeling sadness and despair. If I began to feel this way, he would win, proving to himself, if not to me, that he was "smarter" than me, that there was no one who could help him and that here on earth I, as "God's representative", had not succeeded in helping him, because he had made me despair of ever being able to help him. My despair would mean to him that I would get angry with him because he "wouldn't let me help him". His sadism then became represented in me by my sense of sadness and despair, and I then would become the tyrannically abusive parent in retaliation and continue the sadism. Of course, if I failed him, he would fail also, but that would prove that his "God was powerless" to help him or to want to help him.

As we continued in treatment, he did show some therapeutic gains. He was able to get a job, he began to limit his sexual contacts to a few men, and he began to limit his sexual activity to less dangerous experiences.

However, his therapeutic gain was always very dangerous. It meant to him that he "could be helped", that he could see that there was a glimmer of hope, of life, but this glimmer always set off a tirade of anger towards me: "You're just doing this to prove how good you are. As soon as I trust you, you'll hurt me—you'll leave. You'll tell me I'm fine because I have a job and that I don't need to come here any more." His attacks against his dependency and his attachment to me always brought forth a vitriolic attack on how inept I was, how I did not really understand him, how I forgot some of the things he told me. and how weak I was. "You're just a frail person with no strength who will probably get sick." His projections would make me sick, perhaps literally and physically, and I would be defenceless in the face of this aggression. Then he would prove how "strong" he was by having sexual contact with "hundreds" of partners—all during one weekend. He would return at the beginning of the week looking dreadful, tired, hungry, but jubilant—he had "won" he would tell me. I would interpret his attempts to kill himself so that he would not have to recognize and experience the great pain of his hostility towards his parents, which was now being expressed as anger towards me because he depended upon me. He would tell me that I did not know what pain really was, saying, "You can't think you're so good; you can't help me". I interpreted this as his despair and his anticipation of my rejection of him and feelings. When I told him that I would not "attack" him like his parents and that I would not accuse him of being bad, he usually started to cry and to talk about remembering another physical or sexual abuse experience that had recently begun to surface in his thinking.

As he talked with tears streaming down his face, it became difficult for me not to feel his pain and misery. My interpretation to him indicated that he anticipated that his pain would incapacitate anyone, especially me, from helping him. His response was that "no one cared" and all he could do was to find sexual release from the pain by giving gay men pleasure. He was in control then and was giving something rather than taking something. With me he felt that he was "taking" and that his pain would "wear" me out. Nothing else "mattered", nothing else was "clear". He talked about being driven to die this way, adding that it was punishment from God. "I'm just waiting for it to arrive. No one, not even you can help me, you're not God."

Dying became a conscious desire. Death, he thought, would resolve the difficulties he was experiencing. The expression of his death wish was "dominated by an aggressive part of himself, which attempts to control and destroy my work, but that this part is actively sadistic towards another part of the self which is masochistically caught up in this process, and that this has become an addiction" (Joseph, 1982, p. 450).

Gradually he has been able to see that he is "hooked" on self-destruction and, whenever he makes some gains, both in living arrangements and in treatment, he immediately sets out to destroy those gains. As he explains, "I don't think I could ever be powerful enough to hurt my parents. They always seem to hurt me and if I'm doing o.k., then they'll just come and take everything I have away. They hit me, they abuse me, and they make me feel so awful and bad." He says that he is afraid to change: "I don't know why you think I can change—you must be hooked on proving yourself right and me wrong."

I interpreted this as his despair and his wanting me to continue to feel hopeful yet hopeless at the same time. While he has split off his sense of ever being able to be effectively treated, he sees in me the vestige of help. He has not been able to destroy me or make me feel as inadequate as he feels. He continues to be very frightened by the strength of his anger towards his parents. Periodically he senses how hostile he feels towards them, and for him it is a very physical feeling of anger. As he says, "I can feel how angry I am. It's almost like a thing inside me, and if I actually recognize it, I'm sure it will just get bigger and bigger and destroy me. You won't be able to handle it. It's bigger than you."

He can tell me how angry he is with me, how he now recognizes that when he and I talk about his anger towards me, he very quickly starts to talk about his parents. He realizes that this is "no accident", and he must "be furious with them because of all those things they both did to me". However, he tries to prevent himself from thinking that he could ever benefit from treatment.

He is so afraid that his anger towards them would be expressed that on one occasion, when he decided that he needed to visit them, to "see what they really look like", he announced upon entering their flat, "The taxi is waiting for me. I have to be at the airport, and I have to leave in ten minutes." He was also afraid that they would "take him over", that is, once again hurt him. During those ten minutes he listened to their tirade of his "worthlessness" but did not express any of his feelings. His hostility and his violence are turned against others, mostly men whom he sees as under his control when they gain sexual pleasure from him. His hostility towards himself is experienced when he uses his penis in a jabbing way, inserting it so violently into another that not only does he bleed, but so does the other person. His penis is the part of his body that has offended, and he treats his penis with a violence that to him is not only sexual but painful. As Betty Joseph (1982) said, "It is very hard for our patients to find it possible to abandon such terrible delights for the uncertain pleasures of real relationships" (p. 456).

CHAPTER SEVEN

The destructive role of envy and its alliance with the death instinct to prevent dependency and successful developmental and therapeutic outcome

E nvy can frequently manifest itself both in ordinary and in pathological relationships, but always in the therapeutic relationship. If envy is not dealt with in an effective way, there is the danger that, in development, the maturing child will experience difficulty in maintaining a helpful dependency upon the mother, and, in treatment, the analytic patient will have difficulty in experiencing a therapeutic dependence. In both maturational or therapeutic situations, successful growth may be arrested, and the death instinct may be strengthened, with consequent potential for ego disintegration and destructive outcomes.

The following is an example of a young child who coped with destructive envy by increasing the libidinal tie to the real mother in order to maintain a good internal object, thereby strengthening the life instinct and reducing envy and the death instinct.

> Sam, a 4-year-old boy, was having trouble at home. He refused to do anything that his parents asked of him. He usually then became aggressive and belligerent, and then suddenly, as if a "channel was opened", he would begin to

talk about death. His questions were, "Why did Grandpa die? When will Ruth [a female sibling three years his senior] die? Do the trees die? Will Grandma die? Will you [mother] die because you had to go to the hospital? [after his mother had experienced a successful operative procedure]. Tell me, when will Dad die?"

At one point in his flood of questions, he said: "I want us all to die at the same time and I want to be buried with me on top of you and Ruth can be buried on top of Daddy." Perhaps Sam was trying to resolve a difficult oedipal conflict as well as a fear of separation from his mother and family. However, along with this issue there is the suggestion in his remarks that the only way to keep love and hate apart is to die so there will be no more hate, and by being on top of his beloved mother there will only be love. In this way he can keep love and hate apart, and the strength of the libidinal quality becomes increased. This enables him to cope with envy.

Envy is a very destructive force, and, as Rosenfeld points out, "is particularly unbearable to the infantile ego" (Rosenfeld, 1971, p. 172). Sam's anger is expressed as a desire for "all of us to die at the same time", and the death instinct is expressed as destructive anger. The close relationship between the expression of anger and the death instinct is heard in Sam's remarks. Death and anger both create annihilation, yet in Sam's thinking he has discovered a way to grapple with his strong sense of envy.

Sam seems to have attempted to cope with his envy by becoming one with the good, desired, and satisfying object, his mother. By joining with her in death, he has the phantasy that he will never lose her. He will have his mother by being "on top of her", resolving his oedipal desire of having mother, and not "disturbing" father because he gives him Ruth on top of him. Sam gains control of his idealized object without retaliation from father—father is provided with his own sexual object. However, this can only be achieved by dying. Death is the only solution Sam can arrive at. Death in his thinking accomplishes this gratification and yet seems free of the anger and destructive elements that might bring on the death of all these people at the same time.

Klein (1955) pointed out that children struggle not to destroy their objects, their toys—and that they try to keep them, at times wrapping them up in cloth, or paper, or putting them into drawers or "safe places". They keep parts and bits of broken toys in boxes (some keep them in bags), and I have often seen young children going through a box and bag of broken bits, trying to fit pieces together. They work at trying to put the pieces together for long periods, of time and sometimes, when the pieces do not fit together, they cry and throw the pieces away, only to gather them up later. (If the parent thinks that the child has no further use for these pieces and puts them in the waste bin, the child searches for the pieces. In a few instances I have observed children who could not locate the pieces of their toys, and they became very sad after a fruitless search. One 6-year-old child said, "You threw them out just to make me mad", and another said, "It makes me very sad. I needed to fix the toy." By trying to repair the toy, children are trying to make sure that the phantasied internal object does not become an internal persecuting object. Their attempts at reparation of the toys is, I think, their desire to be "good". The broken toys represent the results of their aggressive reactions, now interpreted as aggression towards the external object. The retaliatory aggression from this external object is anticipated as annihilating. If the external object is repaired, the internal object is repaired, and there will be no further retaliation. Children seem to experience broken toys as broken pieces of their ego (Weininger, 1992, 1993).

It is very difficult for the young child who cannot achieve a strong positive dependence upon his internal object and cannot retain this object as gratifying and persistent to deal with the hostile aspects of his personality. The death instinct, the hostile destructive parts of the personality, prevents the integration of love and hate, life and death, dependence and independence. The stronger the death instinct is, the less integration and fusion occurs (Spillius, 1994).

After Sam had told his mother about his burial plans, he said he would not "be angry any more", that he would feel "o.k." because he knew that he wouldn't be "dead", he'd "just pretend", but that he would "have Mummy whenever I need Mummy—it would be like I could put you on like my jacket".

Sam's aggressiveness was perceived as dangerous, not only to himself, but also to his mother and family. He was sure his destructive impulses would result in retaliation and that he would be destroyed. He found a creative way to deal with this serious issue and perhaps also to deal with the strong envy and oedipal conflict because he saw his father as "having Mummy to himself all the time". By giving father his sister, he intended to placate him and to defuse his father's retaliation for taking his mother for himself. He would become his mother's husband. He was able to overcome the destructive death part of his ego, not by maintaining a split between good and bad ego, but rather by increasing the strength of his libidinal love, creating a way that his dependency would be acceptable to himself. He could "wear" her as a "jacket"—a safe, protective jacket—and in this way always have the introjections of goodness without fearing the envious hostile attacks he might make on the good object. Death and dying was then seen as good and not destructive. Dependency and independence could be integrated, and he would maintain a sense of ego preservation, even in the face of his future refusals to do everything that his parents might ask of him.

As Klein (1958) points out, by feeling less envy, the child is able to introject an object that is "largely in the service of the life instinct: it combats the death instinct because it leads to the ego taking in something life-giving (first of all food) and thus binding the death instinct working within" (p. 238). Klein (1957a) and Rosenfeld both point out that in splitting, the aim is to protect the ego and object "from the danger of annihilation by the destructive impulses deriving from the death instinct" (Rosenfeld, 1971, p. 172). But if the child can fuse the two instincts, life and death, then the dangers of annihilation would be overcome. If this means that Sam has to join the two instincts by death—then, while he does so at this time, in a dissociated thinking way, he does so in an effort to preserve himself.

A 6-year-old boy I know was having a violin lesson. He enjoys the violin and practices whenever he seems to have a "free moment". He is an active, energetic, very likeable young boy, and he wants to play the violin perfectly. During the lesson, his teacher kept reminding him to keep his "first two fingers down"—the correct fingering position on violin strings. The boy said he was keeping his fingers down, and, when reminded to do so by the teacher, he repeated that his fingers were down. Eventually, he said that he wanted to leave and that his lesson was finished. After several remarks about his fingers by the teacher and his mother who was present at the lesson (these remarks were given in a teasing, friendly way, such as: "Your fingers just want to go up in the air" or "Your fingers need a weight on them to keep them down"), he ended the lesson earlier than usual.

He seemed happy, and he talked about his fingers and the lesson. He said that his fingers were "really down, Mum". Following this, he was going to his gymnastics lesson, also a favourite activity. Arriving at the gym, he jumped out of the car and ran to the gym, anxious to change his clothes and be ready for the tumbling and running activity.

His mother and I got out of the car and made our way into the gym. As we entered the gym, we could hear him crying loudly, and we rushed to see him sitting on the bench clutching the fingers on his left hand. The heavy door to the entrance to the gym room had closed on his two fingers—the same two fingers that did not stay down! A man was sitting beside him, but the boy refused to accept any help from him.

His mother and he rushed off to the water fountain to let cold water run over his fingers. He was crying loudly, saying, "It hurts a lot", and his mother repeated, "That was a bad door that hurt you." A few minutes after his mother had repeated her remarks about the door, he stopped crying and said, "Doors don't think, it was my fault." His mother smilingly responded, "Guess even kissing your fingers won't help." The boy said, "No", adding, "It hurts, and it's my fault." His fingers were not lacerated, and after a few minutes he said that it was time for him to go back to the gym. He decided that he would do the tumbling and running but not do any work on the parallel bars.

This child' s ego was sufficiently mature to encompass the pain and the hurt as self-inflicted. He did not need to imagine that it was the "bad door" that had done this damage to him or to phantasize that it was his mother's retaliation for the anger that he must have felt at her teasing him and allowing the teacher not only to tease him but also to contradict him when he said his fingers were "down". I think he wanted to end the lesson at the first indication that he was not playing the violin correctly, and he could not. When he had to continue, the anger he must have experienced was dissociated and split off from the ego in order to protect his ego, his mother, and his teacher from the strength of his anger. The anger remained split off and might have resulted in a poor gym lesson and continuing regression to earlier, more persecutory states.

However, he was able to integrate the anger as being his by saying the hurt fingers were his fault. He did not project it to the bad door, nor to his mother. He was able to recognize that it was his "carelessness" that caused the pain to his fingers—the same fingers that had brought on his anger during the lesson by not keeping "down". The door closing on these two fingers was "punishment", not from the regressive persecutory position of a retaliating mother, but from his own sense of being very angry and not having dealt with the lesson event adequately. Punishment was not just to remind him to keep the two fingers "down" but the harsh voice of his superego. He had to learn to keep his fingers "down", but he also had to recognize that this criticism was not retaliation from his mother and teacher—that they were not angry with him for not doing something "right". He was angry with them and with himself and viewed the criticism as retaliation for his anger—as if keeping his fingers in the wrong place was symbolic of his anger.

I think Rosenfeld described this young boy's situation very clearly when he wrote about narcissism:

> In my previous work on narcissism (Rosenfeld, 1964) I stressed the projective and introjective identification of self and object (fusion of self and object) in narcissistic states, which acts as a defense against any recognition of separateness between the self and objects. Awareness of separation immediately leads to feelings of dependence on an object and therefore to inevitable frustrations. However, dependence also stimulates envy, when the goodness of the object is recognized. Aggressiveness towards objects therefore seems inevitable in giving up the narcissistic position and it ap-

pears that the strength and persistence of omnipotent narcissistic object relations is closely related to the strength of
the envious destructive impulses. [Rosenfeld, 1971, p. 172]

The young boy's lesson did not go "properly" that day, and his
aggression towards mother and teacher was controlled and expressed only as a continued inability to keep his fingers "down"
on the violin strings. The aggression remained, and mother was
not strong enough to keep his fingers down. The separation from
this good object resulted in a temporary state of envy and its
related destructive and retaliatory phantasies. He wanted her
help, and he experienced her teasing as anger. He felt his sepa-
rateness and, at the same time, his desire for the goodness of
the mother to make everything go well. The envious destructive
impulses were expressed as self-destructive finger hurt, not with
accusations of, "It's your fault mother" but, rather, as "It's my
fault." In this way, he could reintegrate the libidinal dependent
ego, accept her help (not someone else's) and "mitigate the destructive impulses" (Rosenfeld, 1971, p. 177).

There seems to me to be a difference in the way individuals
talk about how they consider that things are valuable to them
because they can control them completely, in contrast to others
who talk about things as being valuable because others think of
them as valued. Valuing an object is important in order to
protect a good internal object, and to maintain its protective
value to the person. At times, when its value becomes doubtful,
the person may need to hold it and to rub it as a talisman, or
perhaps to prove to oneself that it is under the individual's
"control". This control is felt by showing the valued object to
another and asking for the other to express a sense of awe about
the object.

However, if envy is felt to be so strong as possibly to destroy
the value of the object, then the person himself will devalue it.
The devaluation is to make the object less enviable. However, at
the same time the individual's sense of well being is reduced—a
sense of not feeling as good because of a sense of internal
deprivation or loss (Weininger, 1992).

When a young boy of 5 noticed that all his playmates wanted
his toy engine, he turned his back on the small group and

broke one of the wheels on the engine. Then he turned to the group and said, "You won't want to play with this broken engine now", and the child had tears in his eyes. He could not cope with the envy of the others, and to reduce the envy he destroyed his toy engine. In doing so, he must have felt as if he had broken a part of himself. Perhaps the part he might have felt he had broken was the envied part of himself, but his hostility towards the group had also been stopped. By breaking the toy, he had reduced their envy of his valued object, but his hostility, expressed as breaking his engine and directed at himself, was at least temporarily blocked.

One of my patients talked about how he would feel angry towards his mother; he said, "Every time I say to myself, or out loud to you, that I am angry with her, something happens to her". I think he was referring to the idea that if he did not consider her as valuable and did not do something to protect her, then she would become ill or have some other kind of problem, such as losing her keys. He went on to say that if he thinks angry thoughts about her, then that means that he must not think she is such a good person. He could not be angry with just something that she did. To him this means he must be angry with "all of her and everything that she does".

During one of our sessions, he told me about an event that had happened to him when he was 10 years old. He was at school and was coming home with his homework when a group of boys, also from the same school, met him and began to taunt him, calling him a "sissy" and a "mama's boy". Then they began to make vulgar remarks about his mother—as he said: "They began to tell me that she is a whore, that she fucks dogs, that she sucks pricks." As he was talking, he became very upset, very red in the face, and very agitated physically. He also seemed to want to get up and move around. He continued to tell me about this horrible incident and how he had managed to get home and did not have a fight with any of the boys. Upon arriving home, he said, his mother had not made her usual snack for him, and he began to feel very angry and told himself that the boys he met were "probably right". As his anger against his mother became stronger, he felt that she was no good and that he did not love her.

His mother told him how tired she was and that she was going to have to go to bed early and that he would have to make dinner for the family that evening. Now he was sure that he was very bad, that he had caused her tiredness, and that he should have been able to fight the boys at school. He was certain that she was not well because he had had "bad thoughts" about her and began to see her as sick because he was a very "nasty person". I think that his valuable object became less valued as others devalued her, and his original hostility towards her could only be controlled when another would talk of her as good. He noted that when his sister and brother and father came home and talked about how kind, loving, caring, and responsible she was, he began to feel better about her. Their words began to reinstate her as a good internal object, and the destructive elements within his ego could be controlled. Once again he became the loving, caring, responsible son and did the evening's work.

Now at age 45 he once again began to feel "out of control" and to feel angry with his mother. He sought treatment because his wife did not think very kindly about his mother, and he did not know what to do about his own feelings of "upsetness", which seemed to come on when his wife spoke poorly about his mother.

During treatment, he explored his anger and his dependency on her, and, on one occasion when he expressed considerable anger towards her because "she controlled me in everything I did", she became very ill shortly thereafter and was hospitalized. He, of course, blamed himself, as he had when he was 10 years old, only this time he accused me of being "just like those boys who told him his mother was bad, and I had no right to do this". He described himself as suicidal and that his death would be the only way his mother would be able to recover from her illness. Suicide would be an ideal way to prevent him from becoming angry again, and he "would have to kill myself very soon because she is getting worse". I pointed out that suicide was a violence both to himself and to his mother as well, and that this violence would leave a wide trail of destructiveness. Suicide as a method of curbing aggression would not work. I also pointed out that his anger against himself would be experienced by his children, who, in turn, would have to deal with their anger towards him because he left them and who might think he did not love them.

I interpreted his difficulties in being able to recognize his anger towards his mother, his fear that she would become ill when he was angry, and how, when others said that she was good, he could reinstate her as a good object. As long as he thought she was good, she *was* good, and his feelings did not harm her. In fact, he was not even aware of these angry feelings.

His hostility could not be contained when someone else did not see his mother as valued. His unconscious destructive impulses towards her and himself could only be contained when he heard that others viewed his identification with her as an ideal identification with a good object. In this way his destructiveness was omnipotently controlled by the other-valued internal object.

In contrast to this other-valued internal object, I think there is also the individual who "takes over" others, internalizes his phantasy of their valued objects as aspects of his own, and then sees no need to be with others.

Whenever Klaus, a 40-year-old man, began to feel dependent upon me, he had to devalue our work and minimize his dependency on me. As he said, "Whenever I begin to feel like I can't miss the session, I know it's time for me to review what we have done and to realize that we haven't done very much. I'm sure I could do whatever you think we've done for me on my own."

It is very difficult for him to begin to recognize this as a feeling of dependency (Weininger, 1993). Whenever he begins to feel dependency, he begins to feel that he is weak, and he can then be manipulated by the other. He is so sure that he will be "used" by another person that he seeks out people to manipulate "first". He deliberately sets himself up as a friend to another person, and, when he thinks that the other person likes him well enough, he leaves him. He also tells me he wants to make sure that he recognizes how "badly the person feels when he leaves him". In other words, my patient sets out to gain another person's friendship, and then, when friendship is achieved, he leaves the person and in this way forces himself to recognize that it is futile to depend on another because "all that happens is that you just get hurt" and "I won't let that happen to me."

In these patients the destructive impulses have become defused (unbound) so that they actively dominate the entire personality and all the relationships a patient has. In analyses such patients express their feelings in an only slightly disguised way by devaluing the analysts' work through persistent indifference, tricky repetitive behaviour, and sometimes open belittlement. [Rosenfeld, 1990, p. 109]

This spoiling of the therapeutic relationship by trying to destroy the dependency state is in order to prevent the pain and hurt he experienced in relations with his parents when he felt they had not met his needs and had "deserted" him because he was not strong enough for them. He must think of himself as being fully independent, even though the object has been introjected. The introjected parent, if realized or recognized, will only be a deserting object, one that will leave and hurt him as the (parent-)object leaves. In this way the patient must not realize the introjected object by never recognizing dependency. He must always think of himself as independent. The introjected parent-object is not simply a part of himself but a part of himself that must remain unrecognized, and, if recognized, then dependency will occur. This unrecognized parent-object introject is maintained by not becoming dependent. The parent as a satisfying object will once again be capable of hurting the child by leaving him alone.

Interestingly, whenever my patient's business dealings begin to become successful, he begins to spoil this potential success. He begins to imagine that he will become dependent upon other business people, who, in turn, could hurt him and manipulate him because, as he says, "They will know that my success is dependent upon their supplying me with the raw goods." Success, dependency, and being cared for by another become extremely difficult for him to endure, and, rather than experiencing these feelings, he destroys the possibilities of their occurrence. Should he begin to feel attracted to one person and want to be with that person, he deliberately begins to seek out "one-night stands" and tries to make sure that his possible partners will either be told about his promiscuous behaviour or, "better still, see me with another partner".

This person needs to think that he is a "self-made person" and that no one but himself is responsible for his success. Rather than realize dependency, he will try to spoil relationships, business success, and educational knowledge. He must "make it on his own" and must not recognize the introjected objects. The hostility towards the introjected objects is too great, as is the fear of retaliation. The harshness of the superego is experienced by the strength of his avoidance of others, and by his spoiling business and educational successes.

As Heimann (1952) pointed out, "He can independently produce his own gratification" (p. 146). The ego he loves is the ego he produced. He can care for himself and needs no one but himself. To begin to realize that he has truly incorporated part-objects that can provide gratification leads my patient to contemplate "the best way to kill" himself.

The recognition of the strength of the destructive envy of the introjected object remains split off and is maintained as split off by a sense of "being able to take care of myself without needing anyone". However, the capacity of my patient to take care of himself is very poor. He eats very poorly, he sleeps very little, and, if he is tired, he does not try to rest; if he feels ill, he does not visit a physician. Without awareness, his ego is identified with the strong destructive envy, and death lurks just around every potentially successful corner. He will destroy himself, and thereby destroy his dependency, which, then, destroys forever the infantile dependency he felt as a baby and young child.

As I see it, the transference problem that must be worked through is to enable him to re-experience this very early dependency, which, I think, was directed primarily towards his mother, without the sense that she will either hurt him by leaving him or hurt him by punishing him for being dependent. He will achieve this sense of dependence with the therapist as he recognizes that the therapist neither leaves him nor criticizes him but remains stable and alert in spite of the dire threats that he makes, such as: "I'll kill myself", "I won't pay you", "I'll make sure everyone knows you can't help me", etc. The transference dependency must contain the destructive envy, not only through interpretation, but also through pointing out concrete examples and/or demonstrations of his attempt at devaluation, of spoiling his business, education, and interpersonal relationships, and of the non-caring for himself. The attempt is to have the therapist become "fed-up" and doubtful as to the efficacy of treatment and to express a sense of hopelessness (Joseph, 1982). In this way the patient's envy would be reduced, and the therapist would be useless. However, in this patient, his sense of superiority was short-lived, because he became aware of how he was trying to destroy me because he was beginning to depend upon me.

My patient did try to destroy the transference dependency, but the interpretation of envy and the concrete examples of how he tried to make me weak and less important to him, as he had done with other people in his life, gradually changed his view of the world as a cruel, manipulative place. He began to recognize that, in spite of his sense that I was "now in charge of the treatment", he wanted to continue on in treatment. He said he was beginning to feel a "joy" in being able to talk about these things, but he was not entirely prepared to give himself over to treatment. As he said, "You'll have to work very hard to prevent me from sabotaging treatment."

> The patient becomes gradually aware that he is dominated by an omnipotent infantile part of himself which not only pulls him away towards death but infantilizes him and prevents him from growing up by keeping him away from objects who could help him to achieve growth and development. [Rosenfeld, 1971, p. 176]

The patient who feels that he is becoming weak because of a sense of dependence upon the therapist also begins to sense a desire for, and envy of, the capacities and strengths of the therapist (which means that these capacities are not present in the patient). The therapist has to be spoiled or the patient thinks he has to destroy himself because he cannot tolerate the growing sense of these unattainable capacities. Death would be preferable to the full realization of his weaknesses, and to allow the dependence to grow would mean being controlled, manipulated, and used by the therapist who essentially represents the feared and hated, yet desired, parent.

> I hold that anxiety arises from the operation of the death instinct within the organism, is felt as fear of annihilation (death) and takes the form of persecution. The fear for the destructive impulse seems to attach itself at once to an object—or rather it is experienced as the fear of an uncontrollable overpowering object. [Klein, 1946, p. 4]

Envy, as Klein pointed out, is a

> direct derivative of the death instinct. She pointed out that

envy appears as a hostile, life-destroying force influencing the relationship between infant and mother. Envy would also be directed against the effective and good feeding mother. She is the most desired object and contains all the satisfactions and gratifications that the baby would want to contain. [Rosenfeld, 1971]

Envy can lead to such intense rage and fear of retaliation with a sense of ego annihilation, an intense death anxiety, that it cannot be consciously experienced nor tolerated by the ego. Instead, the death wish is projected to another, deflecting the anxiety through the mechanism of projective identification.

One of my patients, a 54-year-old woman, became very concerned that her son would commit suicide. She thought that he seemed particularly upset one evening after he returned from University, but no matter what hour she asked him how he was, he responded that he was tired but not sad, nor upset. Nevertheless, she felt that he was hiding something from her, that he was very upset, and that he was considering suicide. She said she could not really understand why she felt so compelled to think this way, and, even in the face of his insistence that he was fine and only tired, she continued to think he would "suicide in a few days". She found herself very worried and preoccupied; she managed to telephone him several times a day at the University, and she "made sure to be home when he came home". She was prepared to try to stop him from this act, and while she did not question him again as to how he felt, she assumed he was bound to kill himself.

She persisted with this idea for about 10 days, during which her sessions were wholly taken over by her attempt to understand why he was going to kill himself. When I pointed out that perhaps she was projecting her concern about her own life into her son, she stopped talking for several minutes and then began to sob quietly. When she tried to talk, her sobs became loud, but without any word sounds. She could not talk during the session after the interpretation and returned the next day to her session to start with loud sobs; only gradually and slowly did she begin to talk.

She said that she thought that maybe she was the one who wanted to die, that she had not really thought of suicide but that maybe she would soon die of cancer or some other "dreadful disease" (she was not physically ill). She continued to say that she was aware of feeling numb and was very disturbed about the many things she had to do and how little time she had to accomplish them. She thought that my other patients were doing "better" than she was, and that I was becoming disheartened by her progress and rather pessimistic about a "successful conclusion to our work".

She continued to talk about her great desire to be a "complete person", not to be constantly judged as the "imbecile of the family" who was always compared to her brother and sister and "coming out last in everything". She said that she did not do as well as they did in school, but "that is no reason to make me feel so bad and to punish me".

I pointed out her anger at her siblings as well as her feeling that she did not have as much as they had—that is, she thought that they had the skill to be successful but that she did not have these strengths. She began to talk about her anger, but very hesitantly, saying, "When I think I'm getting angry, I begin to feel breathless, just as if I'm about to die from not being able to breathe." Anger was very frightening, and she learned at a very early age that she must not become angry because if she did, she was told "get out of my sight", "go to your room", or "I can't stand you like this".

She now became very aware that, on those occasions when she did go to her room, she masturbated all the while she remained there. She thought that she had not remembered this before because it was too frightening to consider the anticipated consequences and said, "I would have been told that I was very bad and not worth anything—a piece of dirt, if they found this out."

Masturbation became her expression of hostility, her way of destroying her parents for making her feel so bad and unworthy, her way of trying also to destroy her siblings "for having the stuff that made them o.k.". She thought that "maybe I feel so numb most of the time because I don't want to get angry so I won't masturbate. I hold everything in, even my breath, I think."

Indeed, her numbness prevented her from having any feelings whatsoever, either of anger or of retaliation. Her projection of these feelings to her son was so intense that she was forced to begin to explore them in treatment. She had experienced a sense that one of her children wanted to kill himself before, but this feeling had been fleeting and she was able to "shake it" off. This time, however, the feeling was very persistent. Therefore, she now had to explore her anger, as well as her inability to accept any of the satisfactions and pleasures that, I think, she began to realize her son was experiencing. She felt that her son, who in phantasy represented her siblings, was having good experiences, was experiencing happiness and pleasure, and was going to do well. She was once again going to be the "imbecile of the family". Her rage and envy and subsequent death anxiety were too great to contain by herself, and so she projected this to her son; she then experienced this as a dread of his suicidal behaviour. In treatment, the dread that her projection could be real gave her a sense of persecution and guilt that was too much for her to bear alone.

Projectively, I became her persecutory superego. In this role, I was to stop her from expressing her hostility by supporting the compulsive idea of her son's suicide and helping her to create ways in which she could stop him from doing this. I think my patient wanted to live and wanted to feel successful as a parent but was having great difficulty in accomplishing this. She often wondered whether she was doing enough for her children. Her projected death wish was, I think, not simply a wish for the envied siblings to die but, rather, a wish that she did not have to have such feelings at all. She wanted to be rid of the dread of annihilation and its terror and to have feelings of pleasure at being alive. But she could not experience these feelings because they would also contain feelings of anger along with love. Anger was too dangerous for her to experience. This emotion meant that she was bad and deserved to be put into her room alone. However, when alone in her room, she masturbated, and she was sure this act was very bad. She seemed to have no way out except to wish for death, yet she also felt she wanted to live and do things. Perhaps, as Segal (1993) put it: "the operation of the death instinct produces fear, pain and guilt in the self that wishes to live and be undamaged" (p. 59).

My patient was aware of how jealous she was of her siblings, saying, "They got what they needed and wanted, while I had to get everything I needed or wanted in a sneaky way." Her envy was experienced towards her parents—towards her mother in particular, who outwardly seemed to favour her other children. My patient expressed a desire to take the goodness from her mother and to replace "her insides with bad things, so that then she would only give bad stuff to my brother and sister and then maybe I could do things and not be so fearful." She wanted for herself what her mother seemed to be giving away freely to others. She was angry with her mother because she did not feel she received what her siblings received. Envy is composed of hostile feelings bound up, not only with wishes for the death of the envied other, but also with the death of oneself. To destroy the envied object so that the person does not experience envy means the destruction of the original source of life itself. Mother and mother's breast are both the source of life and the source of satisfactions to carry on living—she is the first introject and the first needed object—and the first part-object to be envied and desired.

My patient's early life was full of many difficult experiences with her family—for example, being called the "imbecile", being told that she always took things in a "sneaky" way, never openly, thinking that she was never as good as her siblings and that whenever she felt some "good feelings" she was sure that they would only become bad because "someone would say that I had nothing to feel good about". Her death instinct, her sense of anger, and her sense of perceiving her ego as worthless were severely reinforced by this early environment. Her early object relations strengthened her sense of annihilation, terror, and death and added to her identification as a worthless person. Anger could not be experienced as a conscious ego feeling— rather, it was unconsciously projected. Anger was phantasied as coming from the other, making her feel even less adequate and worthwhile because she could not cope with this anger either. Hate and envy could not be experienced—rather, these feelings became projections to her children. This deflected, for a time, her death anxiety and her own sense of annihilation.

As an awareness of these feelings occurs within the safety of a contained transference relationship, acceptance of these feelings as one's own ego feelings can also occur. In this way, the balance between love and hate can alter so that love can dominate. The ego can then perceive itself as being worthy of satisfaction and gratification, as well as capable of experiencing anger as a part of the ego feelings without having to project it. Persecution and superego inflation need not follow, nor does it become necessary to have another person as the persecuting conscience.

In the case of another patient with whom I have been working for two years, his lack of success and his not becoming more effective than his envied mother kept his superego from annihilating him. My patient became unusually tired and then visibly sleepy whenever he began to talk with me about his mother. Initially, as he began to talk about her, he became more and more excited, and then, when he recognized that he had been talking in an excited way, he "toned" himself down and said that he "really shouldn't be talking about mother, she's always been so good to me, always wanted to help me". Slowly he moved to the point where he began to describe the controlling nature of their interaction. His mother would tell him that he needed to "do more exercise", that he needed "to eat less", that he needed "to give his money away to the starving children of Africa", and that he needed "new clothes". As he began to talk about this, he also began to feel tired and gradually "wound down". He had told me that he was sure he became tired because he had been talking about her in such an "animated way".

I had suggested that he was very angry with his mother for the control that she had exerted over him and for the feeling that she did not think he could do anything which was good enough by himself. She always wanted more from him—for example, to be stronger, to be thinner, to be brighter, to be more successful. When I had interpreted his hostility towards her in this way, he immediately fell asleep. Sometimes he slept for a few moments, at other times for half the session. When he awoke, he would look over at me, smile, and say that he "thought" he must have fallen asleep. He offered no explanation for his sleep and continued to talk about his mother in a chatty way, again talking about how capable she was and how she managed her household so well. However, once again, when I interpreted his hostility, he fell asleep.

I have been able to interpret his hostility to his mother by helping him to talk about how and what he does about her remarks that he should do more exercise or lose weight or make more money. For example, he bought a bicycle that was very expensive and had "many gears". When he told her about his purchase, he also added, "It's too difficult for me to ride." When he told her that he had joined a health club, he added, "This is the tenth one I've joined this year." About his weight, he told her that he was cutting down on how much food he ate, but then he brought a rich cake for dessert to his parents' home. As he became aware of the hostility that he was expressing by doing what she wanted, yet at the same time by adding a component that obviously expressed his rage, he started to feel very tired and to fall asleep, but after several starts and stops he said, "This is too silly and too important for me to fall asleep. I'll walk around the room and talk to you." He "took charge" of the way he would talk to me, and gradually he was able to realize how his hostility was expressed. As he "discovered his anger", he felt more capable and, as he said, "not dead any more".

Tiredness, fatigue, sleeping, and being asleep were recognized as resistance to prevent him from realizing, not only the strength of his anger towards his mother, but also his growing dependency on me. Since his mother had continually refused to allow her son to consider that he was doing something well (when, in fact, he was beginning to do well at work) and since he always tried to please her and never felt he could, he was also sure that I would not think he was doing well and that not only would I attack him for not getting "better" (or for "taking too long to get better"), but I would view his not getting better as hostility towards me.

As I interpreted this to him, his tiredness and sleep during sessions stopped, and he was able to explore more about his relationship to his mother. He found that he considered that she had "everything"—that is, she could manage her household, her husband, and herself, read books, go to concerts, do all these things and never seem to be tired. Furthermore, he found that she could do all this alone. He, on the other hand, could not seem to do these things, and when he did try to do things alone, he felt unhappy. He found that he was envious of her capacity. He wanted to have the kind of detachment he felt she showed, yet he found that he could not do things the way she did or the way he thought she wanted him to, and this made him feel inadequate. His anger towards her remained hidden but was expressed indirectly by a continual "not doing things right". "He swings between omnipotence–helplessness in a black hole 'now', using words and behaviour to signal his conviction that no development is possible" (Eigen, 1995).

The destructiveness of my patient's thinking and behaviour not only kept him from doing "no-thing" and kept his destructive interaction with his mother the same, but his lack of success kept his superego from overwhelming and annihilating him. In a way, by doing "no-thing", he could not harm her, nor could he realize his anger towards her. His harsh superego operated to prevent him from being successful. However, lack of success was beginning to destroy him. His mother was powerful, she was idealized, and she was incorporated into his superego, maintaining and reinforcing his sense of helplessness, which, in turn, prevented any hostility from consciously appearing and being known.

My patient literally felt that his mother lived inside him. He spoke of the way he felt very uncomfortable and tense when, for example, he went to buy an ordinary bicycle. He said that this bicycle was not good enough and would not give him all the exercise he should get. While he felt his mother as a real inner person, with the force to make him get what he thought she wanted for him, he somehow always bought the wrong bicycle. His inner object did not actually help him reach his imagined goal, and so his mother's accusations that he was not good enough were always fulfilled. He did not get the right bicycle, and in this way his superego should not punish him for his desire to be better than mother or as capable as he imagined her to be or for envying her. To be as good as mother meant not to be criticized by her, but that would mean to him that he had robbed her of whatever it was that made her "so great". Persecuting anxiety was averted and annihilation was lessened by buying the wrong thing, by "side-stepping" envy, and by not becoming as good as—or maybe better than—mother.

Meltzer (1968) has pointed out that terror, "whose essential quality, paralysis, leaves no avenue of action" (p. 399) is a rigid destructive impulse that shapes the personality organization and expression. I believe this terror was avoided by my patient because he always seemed to be doing the wrong thing. His phantasy of robbing mother could never be undone and repaired because he continually heard her as being critical and un-accepting of himself, whatever he did. Nothing was done well enough. No reparation could be possible, and his dependence on this unforgiving object would only lead to an even harsher superego. He could only perceive her as a good and knowledgeable mother who was unavailable to him. He remained safe as long as he remained omnipotently helpless, yet by being so he became his own tyrant. He could then not express any anger—rather, he fell asleep.

> It is important to note that while the tyrant may behave in a way that has a resemblance to a persecutor, especially if any sign of rebellion is at hand, the essential hold over the submissive part of the self is by way of the dread of loss of protection against the terror. The dread felt in relation to the tyrant is fundamentally a dread of loss of the illusory protection against the terror and may be seen to appear especially at times when rebellion has been undertaken in alliance with good objects which are then felt to be inadequate or unavailable, as during analytic holiday breaks. [Meltzer, 1968, p. 400]

In the case of my patient, he was not convinced at first that our relationship could ever be strong enough or sufficiently containing so as to prevent his death. Sleep was his way of resolving and escaping his terrible dilemma.

* * *

As some people imagine that their parent or parents reside in themselves, others imagine that their parents have taken things that belong to others.

The following conversation was recorded by James' mother, a student of mine. James, a 4-year-old boy, was looking down his mother's blouse, and his mother asked him what he was looking for. James answered, "your penis". A second time, when James was again looking down her blouse, she felt that she was better prepared to talk to him about his search:

MOTHER: What are you looking for?

JAMES: Your penis.

MOTHER: Is it my penis or Daddy's penis?

JAMES: Daddy's penis.

MOTHER: How did I get it?

JAMES: You cut it off Daddy.

MOTHER: Is it a good penis or a bad penis?

JAMES: A bad penis.

That James imagined she had a penis and that she took it from his father and that it was a bad penis is one indication of an object (a part-object) residing in another object. James, I think, was expressing some of his oedipal anxieties and was being very expressive about his relationship with his mother. Perhaps James was imagining the fearfulness of his mother's body, a place of destroyed and vengeful part-objects that could damage him as well.

James, however, unlike my patient, has introjected a kind and nurturing mother:

MOTHER: Do you have a Mummy inside of you?

JAMES: Yes.

MOTHER: Is it a good Mummy or a bad Mummy?

JAMES: A good Mummy.

MOTHER: What does she do?

James: She gives me her nipple to suck [*at this he slipped his thumb into his mouth and began to suck*].

CHAPTER EIGHT

Finishing therapy:
one session after three years
of treatment with a patient
who is setting a date
for termination of treatment

We have been talking about stopping the sessions, and Tom, age 32, has said that he wants to set a date to stop but that he is having great difficulty doing that. He talked about being able to do so much more, about being able to have an enduring relationship with another person, a relationship that has lasted and "looks like it will last" for a lot longer. He had not been able to have such a relationship before, and this relationship has been going on for almost two years. In the past he noted that he had not been able to keep a job, and now not only has he been able to keep his job for over a year, but he has been promoted to manage the store. He talked about being able to plan to leave his job for a better job, that he could accept a lower salary because he could see that he was going to be able to learn more in the new position and the new job offered more advancement. He felt that he could now think about the future and he was not afraid to do so.

He had gone for interview and had been hired. He had felt very pleased that he was hired and pleased that he could put himself in the position of having to prove himself. He has been in his new job for 12 months. Recently, he was asked to consider an interview for a managerial position at his place of work. He was surprised to find that not only could he think about a promotion, but he was enjoying the idea of "thinking about it" and perhaps of becoming a manager. Generally, he is well, he does not suffer from the physical problems he experienced in the past, and emotionally he finds that he is able to cope with "difficulties". He now gets along with his family and realizes their difficulties without becoming enmeshed in the dynamics of their problems.

Following this recounting of how well he feels he is doing now, Tom said that he did not know whether he could "really set a date to stop the sessions"; he added that he was not "sure that he wanted me to set a date either". He said he wanted to set a date, yet he added that he thought he still wanted me to help.

Tom began to talk about how he used to feel when he thought he was "finishing something". To Tom, finishing something meant that he would die. He talked about not wanting to do his homework at school, about trying to run away so school would not end in the summer, about not wanting anything to stop without "having control over the stopping". Tom wanted to be in charge of everything, including school, his home and parents, his things, and his friends. Because he was not sure whether he could be in charge of these people or·events, he said that he would try to not get "involved", because if he was involved, then they could decide when things would finish, and if things "finished", he was sure he would "die".

When I asked Tom to talk about the words and thoughts "die" and "in charge", he began to talk about his early camping experiences. He said that he had not wanted to go to camp because he was concerned that at camp he would not be in charge. However, gradually he began to recognize that if he was away from home, "everything" might disappear at home, and he was "absolutely afraid" that he "was going to disappear, to cease to exist". If there were no home to count on, there was no way that he could continue to be. He likened this to a tree falling in the forest, and since no one hears it, no one knows that it has happened. If he goes away from home, he would die, and no one would know. He again thought that if he was in charge of how things went on at home and he did not have to leave, he would not die. When he was at camp, he said he was homesick, and this homesickness was felt by Tom as the feeling that he was beginning to die.

Tom then began to talk about his parents and about his belief that his parents would "not exist" without him. He felt they would die if he was not there and that he was responsible for their lives, so he had to be at home to make sure everyone was well. When he began to recognize some of the paradox of his words—that he would die if he left home and that they would die if he left home—he then said, "No wonder society invented God— God keeps everyone safe, and you can think of God as protecting you and your parents. It's like you protecting me and letting me talk about all these strange things and finding out that when I talk like this, you don't die, and neither do I. I think I've been angry with everyone and everything, and to make sure nothing happened I couldn't leave home. Maybe my rage would kill them somehow, and maybe if I leave here I'll be so angry with you, that you'll die, or maybe you'll kill me for being angry with you."

"At camp I pretended to be sick, and then I felt I was in charge of me. They couldn't tell me what to do when I was sick. I would decide. I even faked an accident to hurt my arm so I was in charge of me." I pointed out that if he was in charge, he was also in charge of his rage, and no one would get hurt because he felt so angry. He put himself in charge in an effort to both deny and control his rage, which would annihilate others as well as himself.

He then talked about his parents—that they did not give him any "limits at all", and so he continually "tested" to find out how far he could go—but he added that he had to be in charge, in control. At school he also had to be in charge. He said, "Everyone depended upon this." To him this meant that if he was "just like one of the crowd", then he could never "be in charge". So he was different, he did not have any friends, he did not do school-work to "keep up", and he did not listen to the teachers. Others had friends, passed their grades, and listened to the teachers. He said that he had to be in charge, so that he would not have to recognize that he was always so angry. As long as he was in control, he did not feel challenged, and then he never had to prove himself. He was in control of the events and situations and so did not have to recognize his anger. As long as he was in charge, he was in charge of his anger.

When the time came to terminate treatment and to set a final date, at first Tom said that he did not want to "think about that", but gradually he recognized that he could think of it and set a date. He said that if he decided that we could not talk about a date, then he was in charge, and he would not have to realize that separation would mean not only pain and grief, but anger as well. This anger was towards me for helping to bring him to a point where he needed to separate, to leave "home", yet now without the sense that he or I would die. He was separating, but now with the sense that he had "things of his own", that he felt a history of accomplishments, and he would not die. He would feel sad about leaving, and he did not have to hide or cover up this sadness with a sense of anger and a subsequent feeling of annihilation if in fact he left or finished something that could lead to separation. Now that he was doing well, he did not have to be alone, he recognized that he made a contribution when he and others decided what to do or where to go.

Tom was not alone, he left one job to go to a potential better one, he was involved in a long-term relationship, and his relationship to his parents and family were greatly improved. He then said, "With all the work I've done—we've done—and the good feelings I have, I think I'll still be angry that I'm not talking to you. Maybe I've been trying to kill you off—or maybe myself off—so we wouldn't have to finish in a good way. With death there would be mourning, but I wouldn't have to deal with the pain of knowing that you're around."

Tom continued to talk about how in the past he had had to be in charge of his own life—he could not allow himself to feel that someone might help him to achieve or to feel better because that would mean that he was not in charge of events in his life. He wanted to think that he was responsible for "creating" himself, because if he depended on anyone, then he would die, because they could leave him. Depending on someone was too dangerous. They could "control you, manipulate you, and toss you away".

He related this aspect to his parents and felt that since they set no limits for him, he could manipulate things in order to decide what he wanted to do and how and when he wanted to do these things. No one told him what to do, nor did his parents. Thus, in one way he set his own limits, but in another way he did not set limits for himself because he would do some very dangerous things—drive while extremely intoxicated, use drugs, and take unusual chances—but he did these things because, as he said, "I decided to do them."

He then recognized that he would not only do these things as a young man, but he had done many other dangerous things as a child—like climb tall trees or run out into the street—in order "to scare myself". Then, if he could frighten himself, he did not have to realize the intensity of his feelings of rage—rage because he needed limits set by parents. And since they did not set such limits, he "tested the extreme limits", but he found that they still did not intervene. He tried to get them involved, and he would be very angry if they did and very angry if they did not. If he could frighten himself, then he would not realize the intense angry feelings he had—his fright would block out everything else. But he never frightened himself enough, and the danger that these feelings might emerge forced him to leave—to just get away, to "travel", as he said. Now, towards the end of treatment, Tom had become aware of his intense feelings. Stopping treatment felt in a way like finishing school, finishing a course, completing a termpaper—the kinds of events that meant his death.

Now Tom was able to explore these very complex interactions between rage, death, love, work, feelings of closeness, dependency, and being in control or, as he said, "being in charge", as well as the sense of lack of limits set by parents, not finishing exams and courses, and now being able to feel emotions and relationships to others while still feeling a sense of being and living.

* * *

In working through the sense of annihilation, the hostile feelings are moderated by the libidinal aspects of the ego—by the force of the life instinct. The ego survives, not only because it matures but because of the consistency and nurturing of its object relations. The ego can maintain itself because aggression is not perceived as being always bad; some aggression is needed to simply accept what is given or even to ask for what is needed and at times, if necessary, to "fight for what you have".

Normal fusions (of the forces of life and the forces of death) are necessary for working through the depressive position, a process which Melanie Klein regarded as essential for any normal development. However, to establish normal fusions it is clinically and theoretically necessary to uncover firmly and distinctly the confusions of good and bad objects and good and bad aspects of the self, because nothing positive or sound can develop from the confusions, and there is a danger that a permanently weak or fragile self will result. [Rosenfeld, 1990, p. 124]

PART TWO

MANIFESTATIONS
IN OUR COMMUNITY

It's not forever and never again: young children's developmental concepts of death

I had the opportunity to try to understand children's ideas about dying and death when I worked with normal young children; I presented some play materials to them and talked about their ideas that were evoked by our conversations and the play materials. I think that as we engage in such play with children, we will learn more about children's fear, anger, and sense of loneliness when they are separated from people they love and need.

The following is included to illustrate not only what some of the research literature tells us, but also what the children I worked with told me.

One night last spring, when I was discussing my recent work on death and children's thinking about death with a colleague, she related the following incident to me. She was troubled at the difficulty she was having in knowing what to say and how to talk to her 7-year-old son about death. Several days before, her son had informed her that he had to take a flower to school for Sarah because of a very special assembly. As she cut a tulip for him, she asked what this was for and what was the very special assembly. Her son seemed vague, did not answer, and just ran off to catch the bus. In the evening, my colleague attended a parents' night at her son's school, and the teacher informed the parents of the pupils in Grade 1 that Sarah, one of the children in the class, had died over the past weekend, and they had held a special memorial assembly for her that afternoon. All the parents had known that Sarah had bone cancer. The previous autumn, those who had visited the school had seen her hobbling on crutches, a scarf covering her nearly bald head, but with bright, flashing eyes in a painfully thin face. She had come to school only occasionally and was hospitalized frequently, but the teacher still maintained her as part of the class, and in class she was very much a part of the group. The children in her class played with her as though they were unaware of the severity of her illness, and the teacher had noted the children's calm acceptance of her, which was unchanged even after one of her legs had been removed. It was with a wrench at the thought of the springs and autumns she would not have, and with that special moment of thankfulness that I think every parent feels seeing or hearing about a dying child—that it is an ordeal most are not faced with themselves—that the Grade 1 parents sat silent, many in tears. I think that these tears were not just for Sarah— an only child—but for their own vulnerability as parents and for their children, many of whom were now brought for the first time face to face with death.

The teacher related the explanation that had been given to the children that day about death—that Sarah was still there and with them when they played and sang, but now in their memory of the times they had shared; that a body was a kind of little house for the mind and soul, and that often the body just got older and wore out, but sometimes things were wrong with it, even when it was new, or accidents happened to it, and then the little house—the body—died, leaving the soul homeless, except in the memory of those who loved the person.

At that time, feeling the emotion of the shared sorrow over the death of the child and gratitude that her own children were alive, my friend felt that the story was a good one, dodging, as it did, around possible religious differences existing in the school community; but afterwards, at home with her son, she was not so sure and did not know whether to question him or wait for his reactions. Several days passed, and Peter said nothing at all.

She watched him carefully, and he did not seem anxious or sad. She knew that he had been fond of Sarah, had frequently played with her, helped her, and stayed with her at the edges of the playground when she could not climb the hills and run with others, and she knew that he had missed her when she was in hospital. And yet, now she was dead, he did not seem concerned. Finally, she asked him how he felt about Sarah's death, and he replied that it was all right; she had simply "gone away because her house was not all right to live in any more", and she would "be back to sing and laugh with them again". The flower, Peter said, "was to make Sarah feel better and not miss us so much", and death was not "forever and never again". It was just like being sick, he said, "when it was over, Sarah would be all better in both her legs again".

Faced with what she could only see as absolute denial of the reality of death, the mother was very worried. What should she do? What could she do? Could she make him—or should she make him—realize that death was a final separation? Or should she say nothing at all? What answers did she have to questions about life after death? What safety could she provide for him? There really seemed to be no answers. What, she asked me, should she do? Since I had been working with parents of dying children and with the children themselves, I think she thought that surely I must know whether this denial was normal, and how best to deal with children when trying to talk about death.

Probably each of us, either as professionals and/or as parents, has had to try to deal with the anxiety-arousing and emotionally laden subject of death and children. I do not believe there are any easy, pat answers, any simple formulae, that will magically help us—and through us, our children—to learn to accept dying as a part of the process of living. I would like to discuss some of the things I see as problems in this area and some of the information we do have that perhaps sheds some light on this difficult topic.

The roots of our thinking about how to cope with death are, I believe, deep in the fabric of our essentially death-defying society. We have removed old people and sick people from our view as much as possible, and we stress the miracles of modern medicine, which can overcome so many dreaded illnesses. No longer do children grow up with their ageing relatives who die at home. No longer is death a part of life to be expected, if not accepted. It is somehow a failure of the system when someone, especially a child, dies. From my discussions with them, this seems to be especially true for those in the medical profession. Often to these people, and no doubt to others, death seems almost a personal enemy, to be fought in non-stop battles of a very long war, and the losses are very hard to accept.

It is also a trying and emotional time for parents of terminally ill children, or children who die as the result of accidents. Many of them feel tremendous amounts of guilt. Perhaps there is something they could have or should have noticed earlier and done sooner. This guilt often has devastating effects on their relationships with each other, with the dying child, and with the child's siblings, both at the time of the crisis and for some time after that. The parents often feel "totally without resources" for dealing, not just with their children and the dying child, but with each other. It would seem, from many cases with whom I have worked and from what has been written, that many of the medical professionals are also fighting personal reactions to the death of the child and are often unable to support parents or the dying child and help them at this very difficult time.

Compounding this distancing from death as a personal experience in our society is an overwhelming preoccupation with violent death. Even very young children are exposed, almost daily, to violent television cartoons (fictionalized, but with very graphic army, police, and emergency people) and television newscasts with gory footage of factual carnage and world-wide disasters. Children are exposed to huge front-page pictures of fatal automobile and plane accidents, fires, and wars. When children wince and express anxiety about these media deaths, they are often told that it is not real: "Don't worry, he is just pretending to be dead", or "Never mind, it's a long way away, and it won't happen to us here." In our desire to protect our children from the realities of human violence, warfare, and misery, and from the fantasies created about these realities for the "entertainment" (which seems to me somehow an inappropriate name for such programming), we are further confusing the issue for young children. Young children often have a very blurry, fuzzy line between what is fantasy—for example, the tooth fairy, the Easter Bunny, and other assorted pleasant make-believe and magic people or characters—and what is reality. When we tell them that those people they see shot to pieces and bleeding are just pretending, as in the films, we are obviously adding something to their unreal conception of death. We are supporting their fantasy that dead people "come alive" and "do things" again.

The results of this societal, professional, and personal confusion and anxiety about death are clear in the way we talk about it, feel about it, and work it through as individual adults. It is very hard for each of us to think about death, and many of us do not, until we have to deal with the personal experience of the deaths of our own parents; this, then, so often leaves us shaken and with a deep sense of abandonment, no matter what our age. It is not an easy or painless process for anyone. Even the possession of a deep and abiding religious faith in an after-life does not numb the pain of loss and separation from loved parents. We mourn, of course, not just for the person who is gone. We mourn for ourselves, for the times not to be shared, and, if we are honest, we are angry, too, at the person who is dead for abandoning us, much in the same way as the young child, whose mother leaves the room temporarily, gets into a rage as if she had left for good. Very few of us can really think with equanimity of our own death. We seem to be protected by the thought that comes into our heads: "It can't happen to me." "It won't happen to me." Adult patients with terminal illnesses often speak of their disbelief at the diagnosis, and they refuse to accept that the dying process is now happening to them. This is followed by their rage and then their sense of "Why me? What have I done that I deserve to die?" For many people, the ending of life is thought of as the work of God. Perhaps this is a residue from the traditional, rather judgmental view of death as retribution for sinners and as the wrath of God. This is often followed by a depression and then resignation. No one can "fight" God—but everyone can ask for a miracle from God.

It is not to be wondered at, therefore, that we have trouble talking with our children about death, or talking with other people's children, and especially working with dying children. Our own fear of loss and need for comfort and safety, our desire to protect the young from pain which we already know we cannot do, our frustration at not being able to defeat death, all get in the way of talking to children about death, and often our feelings really complicate the situation. At times we give too much information to some, frightening the child whose question was not that all-encompassing. Perhaps, in trying to allay their anxiety, we make death sound very lifelike, attributing very worldly qualities to the after-life we describe. The best example of this, of course, is the picture of a white and shiny Heaven, with gold-winged angels sitting on clouds, playing harps, and singing happily, and a dead parent or sister or brother going there to live with God, a very gentle, white-bearded old man. At times we hear the words children say about death, and we assume that they understand their own words, when really they are only parroting words from the media or from adults. We react to the words we hear from the child; we do not consider whether the child actually understands these uttered words. In fact, I think that we often tend to forget that children are not little adults. Children do not have concepts and understanding like ours, nor do they experience fears, anxieties, and mourning in the way we do. In the same way that they develop the rest of their cognitive abilities, children gradually develop accurate concepts about life, death, and immortality. If we do not recognize this, we make it harder for ourselves and much harder for the children to understand these difficult concepts. Often children catch from us a sense of deep fear and anxiety—perhaps the shocking recognition that the adults in their lives are afraid of the subject of death itself.

Since much of the work and writing done by myself and others on the subject of the development of children's concepts about death shares a general psychological grounding in the works of Piaget, I will review very briefly what I consider to be the stages of intellectual development. It is important to remember that stage development theory postulates that these stages always come in order, but not always at the same chronological age in every child, and they are not always complete for all areas of thinking. Development is related not only to age, but to biological growth patterns, to home and family background, and to the totality of life experiences the child has had up to that point. In other words, nature and nurture are important aspects to consider in stage development theory. It is also important to realize that children's thinking often regresses during periods of stress, and children, as well as adults, show thought processes that may then be ascribed to younger ages. In other words, it is always important to regard thinking and intellectual development as flexible and not rigid, in much the same way that Klein described "positions", rather than "stages", in emotional and psychological development (Weininger, 1992).

Stage 1: The sensory-motor stage in many children operates from birth to about 2 years of age or to the onset of functional language. In this stage, thought is pre-verbal, and the child deals with the environment through schemas. Gradually, through sensory and motor experiences, the child realizes that the environment has properties of space, location, permanence, and causality. Behaviour is directed towards need satisfaction through continual testing of the environment by manipulation, exploring, grasping, tasting, and touching. Children know about things, people, and animals but cannot yet transform their knowledge into spoken language in precise ways.

Stage 2: The pre-operational stage seems to have two sub-stages: pre-conceptual from the age of 2 to about 4 years, and intuitive thought from the age of 4 to about 7 years. In the first sub-stage, the child develops the ability to imitate the behaviour of those people not present. His reasoning is neither inductive nor deductive but pre-conceptual, moving from one instance to another without necessarily making any connections or distinctions. In the second—the intuitive thought sub-stage—the child constantly reconstructs mental images of personal experiences with people, animals, and things and acts them out. The child seems to have an intuitive grasp of situations and of cause and effect and feels and senses a great deal that cannot yet be articulated clearly with language. The child literally knows more than he can tell. There are gaps in his reasoning, and misinformation often fills them as he attempts to explain things. He is egocentric, seeing himself as the centre of the universe. The child's language skills are developing rapidly, as is the connection of language with thought and action. He is learning to anticipate and become less impulsive and to reflect and suspend judgement temporarily. Paradoxically, although thinking is ahead of language skills, the child often talks about events and people as if he understands a great deal. For example, a young child can tell an adult, "It's cold because it's dark", but further questioning reveals that the parroting of words heard from the adult lacks concrete reference. She says, "I know it's cold at night because my Daddy told me to put my jacket on. He said it was cold at night and it was dark." No reference is made as yet to the lack of sunlight. Many of our assumptions about what children understand about death are based on such second-hand verbalizations of overheard conversations.

Thus, the pre-operational child operates with what Piaget calls "pre-concepts"—that is, concepts that are partial and ill-defined. The child does not as yet abstract, infer about, or evaluate ideas drawn from his environment. He may know that Tuesday follows Monday and Wednesday follows Tuesday, but not that Wednesday follows Monday, even if he can reel off the names of the days in order.

Stage 3:   Concrete operational thought is present from about 7 to 11 years. In this stage, logical operations are concrete because they are tied to direct experience and based on concrete matters. The child has begun to develop logical thinking and the ability to appreciate the meaning of rules and to apply them voluntarily and, usually, appropriately. Logic now depends on thought rather than on perception alone. Important for our understanding of the child's concept of death is the fact that at this stage the child can grasp reversibility in the physical world. With varying degrees of sophistication, the child can engage in problem-solving requiring planning, relating, classifying, and drawing conclusions.

It is important to remember that although these stages are considered to come in a somewhat fixed order at non-fixed ages, children may be in transition between stages. During such times, early stable concepts and thinking skills are being replaced by new, as yet unstable ones that, in times of stress, may be given up for the familiarity of the older thought patterns, just as new patterns of behaviour may be given up temporarily at such times.

Also important is the recognition that concepts develop from many experiences. Young children's concepts are mostly incomplete and inaccurate because they have been built on limited time and experience. Much of their learning derives from daily incidents, which, for their own reasons, have appeared as significant for them and which are incorporated into their play and sometimes into their conversations, until they are understood. Learning is the discovery of personal meaning. Each child organizes learning logically for himself, according to his or her experiences and intellectual abilities and the way that these are personally perceived. Given this basic assumption, it is easier to understand how widely one child's knowledge about, and understanding of, any experience may vary from another child's of the same age and intellectual capacity. So it seems to be with the concept of death.

Several people have extended Piaget's (1951) developmental theory regarding the conceptualization about conservation, seriation, cause and effect, reversibility, and probability to a conceptualization about life and death. Piaget himself claimed that the concept of death is not established until the pre-pubertal or pubertal years. He was not, however, directly concerned with the concept of death but, rather, with animism—a developmental concept according to which children at first attribute life to everything and then gradually restrict it to animals and plants. Thus, he was dealing with the child's concepts of consciousness and life. It seems obvious to me that a concept of living is necessary before a concept of dying can develop (Safir, 1964).

The existing research on children's understanding of death shows some basic patterns of development closely related to age and suggests some of the ways in which characteristic ideas about death and dying may be influenced by particular cultural and psychological circumstances (e.g. Anthony & Bhana, 1988–89; Mikulincer, Florian, & Tolmacz, 1990; Orbach, 1988; Wenestam, 1984). The pioneering studies of Piaget (1951) and Nagy (1948) have strongly influenced the basic approach and particular methods of investigation of later studies. Piaget's work provided the developmental framework for later investigations. His broad exploration of the relationship between the concepts of animism and death was done by administering ten stimulus words orally to each of thirty children in three age groups, questioning whether each stimulus was alive, could be hurt, grew up, or died. These questions were followed by interviews exploring the child's rationale for decisions that he made about each stimulus. He found that as their concepts of life improved, so did their concepts of death.

This basic outline of conceptual development has been filled in by studies that concentrate on more specific details of children's responses to ideas of death and dying and attempt to account for their peculiar characteristics. Thus, the methods and results of Nagy's famous study of Hungarian children in the 1940s have been further explored in the work of such investigators as Rochlin (1959) and Gartley and Bernasconi (1967) in the United States.

Nagy (1948) studied children ranging from 3 to 10 years of age, who were asked to write down anything about death and to explain their ideas. In interviewing the children, Nagy asked, "What is death?" . . . "Why do people die?" . . . "How can one recognize death?" . . . "Do you dream about death?" She found three basic stages of development characterized by specific forms of response. In children between the ages of 3 and 5 years, there was a denial of death as a regular and final process. It was a temporary state with degrees of death. Researchers have since found that youngsters between the ages of 3 and 7 believe that the dissolution/cessation of life occurs in a sequential manner, the mind being the last thing to go (Hoffman & Strauss, 1985). These children knew that they were alive, but they also imagined that dead people were alive—they did not distinguish between living and not living. Speece and Brent's (1984) position is similar in that they caution against crediting children with more knowledge than they actually possess. For example, they report that young children fail to view being dead or alive as distinct states. Between the ages of 5 and 9 years, for children death becomes personified. Death becomes a person who walks around trying to catch people and carry them off. There seems to be an invisible struggle with death, as if the person who does not get away would die. It seems that children at this age think of death as an external agent. At about the age of 9 years, children begin to think of death as brought about by an internal process that is inevitable, permanent, and irreversible.

Gartly and Bernasconi (1967) interviewed 60 Catholic school children and did not find either reversibility or personalization. They did, however, find that the idea and concept of death standardized with increasing age. They point out that religious training and exposure to television may have acquainted the children they studied with views of death that had in the past been unavailable to children, and that they might be verbalizing what they knew adults wanted to hear rather than what the children really knew.

Gregory Rochlin (1959) pursued Nagy's investigation with 3- to 5-year-olds and corroborates the latter's findings with his work with American children. These children find death reversible—that is, when someone dies, he continues to grow, get hungry, eat, and move. Rochlin felt that while young children are cognisant of the recognition of death as the absence of life, they do not philosophically accept this fact due to psychological defences that are magically related to their sense of omnipotence and invulnerability (Rochlin, 1959). The defence against such a loss as would be realized by an accurate awareness of death would be a sense of annihilation. Rochlin related the rejection of death as the absence of life to Freud's ideas about narcissism as an explanation for children's denial and refusal to accept the finality of death. This early age-group has a belief in omnipotence, wishes, and the power of magic and shows an imperishable egocentricity, as well as a sense of helplessness, coupled with dependence on those in authority and a deep and pervasive concern with causality. The phantasy is of an internal protective object. To change this phantasy, the child needs sufficient good-enough experiences with the adults in her life so as to experience an internal ego that can master bad "things". Young children, I think, are unsure as to the strength of their ego in overcoming bad events, and, rather than experience the anxiety of annihilation, children deny the concept of death as permanent and irreversible. The denial seems to be important to the children because the death of someone or something is often experienced as the child's fault: "If I had been better, my parent wouldn't have died"—and children must defend themselves against subsequent phantasized retaliation.

Young children live in a world that is full of living, acting things, responding to them, amusing them, feeding them. They do not know what it means for life to disappear forever, nor can they theorize where "life" would go. Only gradually do they recognize that there is a thing called death that takes people away forever. Very reluctantly they come to admit that sooner or later death takes everyone away, but the development of this gradual realization of the inevitability of death may not come until the ninth or tenth year.

Kastenbaum (1965) attributes the personification reported by Nagy in children from 5 to 9 as being due to the fact that at this age children can neither deny nor accept death as an authentic aspect of their own lives and so seek a compromise, creating an image or accepting cultural images such as the skeleton man. Death, therefore, is kept remote, outside one's self, something that can be kept at bay through careful living, if not planning.

In the 1970s, several researchers looked at the concept of inevitability, reversibility, and differences between life and death states. Their findings were not dissimilar to what had already been uncovered. In 1972, Hansen used Piaget's stage framework to design a study that showed significant differences between children in 4-to-5, 7-to-8, and 11-to-12 age groups. Pre-school children were seen as conceiving of death as a non-permanent, reversible state that possesses characteristics similar to life; they had no concept of universality or physiological separation. The 7- to 8-year-olds understood death as a definitive state—the termination of life—but, contrary to expectations, seemed to have a grasp of death as an internal corporeal process, and they comprehended the aspect of inevitability. The oldest children studied had acquired a full understanding of dissolution and ideas of reincarnation and body–soul differentiation. Hansen concluded that the notions of classification, conservation, time, and age, acquired in the concrete operational stages, seemed necessary elements for grasping death as a definitive and universal event.

Childers and Wainer (1971), attempting to prove that the cognitive awareness of death as universal and irrevocable and that cognitive understanding is independent of recognizing one concept before the other one, found, instead, that, in fact, the cognitive point for understanding death as universal was after the age of 9 and that through 10 years of age children are unsure about the irrevocability of death.

Formanek (1974) did a research study with almost 300 children and found that, whereas 32% of the children under age 7 knew what criteria to apply to decide what was living, only 6% had an adequate understanding of the word "dead". At the most immature level, children did not understand the question or confused it with the word "death", as if death caused "dead" or vice versa. At this level, death may be the cause of much anxiety, and some considered that a limited understanding of it may be an impediment to successful mourning (Schonfeld & Kappelman, 1990). At the next stage, children gave partial explanations based on information gathered from here and there, with much misinformation and gaps. This is consistent with the stage of pre-operational intuitive thought. In the 7- to 9-year age range, only 20% had achieved understanding of death as both final and universal.

Koocher (1973, 1974a, 1974b) conducted a very thorough study in which the children were tested for level of cognitive development in Piagetian tests and intellectual levels before being given questions to answer about death. The four questions he used were: (1) "What makes things die?" (2) "How do you make things come back to life?" (3) "When will you die?" (4) "What will happen then?" Pre-operational children included fantasy reasoning, magical thinking, and explanations closely tied to their own experiences in the answers to these questions. Generally, these children were under 8 years of age. Concrete operational children within the 7- to 12-year range gave answers that indicated specific means of inflicting death, such as weapons and assaultive acts, rather than general bodily processes. Formal operational children who were mostly 12 years of age gave more abstract clusters of possibilities and recognized physical deterioration and death as a physical process. Only pre-operational children, all under 7, suggested that reversibility was possible, and only these children based their estimates on when they would die largely on fantasy instead of reality and observation of others.

On the question of what happens after death, the range of responses was wide: 52% referred to being buried; hints of after-life such as heaven or hell were given by 27%; reference to funerals was made by 19%. Specific predictions of how death would occur were made by 10%; references to some aspect of sleep by 7%; being remembered by others by 5%; reincarnation by 4%. He found it surprising that little in the way of religious concepts of death and after-life was elicited. Only 7% used the word "God" in answering questions. Koocher suggests that the weight of religious content in most of the children's exposure to death—that is, generally through the media—is almost non-existent, and that this may explain this finding, where growing disillusionment with religion as a mode of coping with death, especially in his university area research population, may be reflected. To me, his most interesting suggestion is that just as it is possible that Nagy (1948) found personification as a coping method for distancing death, so now children are more inclined to use specificity of detail as a means of mastery and, hence, as a means of control of death and of its consequent meaning.

Spinetta (1974) noted that many of the researchers in their studies of children on the concept of death base their conclusions on adult (parental and staff) observations rather than on talking directly with children. Stambrook and Parker (1987) report a more current yet similar finding. In fact, a study conducted in Italy by Vianello and Lucamante (1988) found that parents and paediatricians alike believe that, under 5, children never think of death and comprehend little of it until they reach 7 or 8 years of age. Furthermore, the majority of paediatricians interviewed (i.e. twenty-seven out of thirty) believed that it was not their function to discuss the matter with their young patients (Vianello & Lucamante, 1988).

It is important, I think, to understand and investigate the child's perceptions of death from his own point of view and concept of the world. Death and the contemplation thereof is something children, even very young ones, experience as part of life (Speece & Brent, 1984). However, this latter point remains unrecognized or disbelieved by some researchers and the lay public (Stambrook & Parker, 1987). By studying children of varying ages and similar socioeconomic backgrounds, I have attempted to enhance our understanding of the developmental aspects of children's knowledge of death. By exploring the ways in which their assimilation of the concepts of "dying" and "dead" are expressed, not only through language but also through play, I hoped to understand more about the internal life of children.

It is equally important to recognize that concepts develop from many experiences. Young children's concepts are mostly incomplete and inaccurate, partly because they have been built on limited time and experience. However, the research literature shows (Stambrook & Parker, 1987) that certain experiences (e.g. terminal illness) can effect a well-developed understanding of death in very young children (also Fetsch, 1986; Krasnow, 1992; Lanzi, Balottin, Bargotti, & Ottolini, 1993; Orbach, 1988). More dramatically, van Eys (1987) and Raimbault (1991) claim that when faced with illness and death, a child will arrive at the same place in his understanding of death by way of the same sequence of conceptual realizations and confusions as does the adult.

Nevertheless, for most normal children not faced with such a drastic event, it is different. Davis (1986) claims that a void exists in understanding how normal children relate to death. Perhaps for children the idea of death acquires meaning as an immediate fact of what makes up the effort of being. Much of learning derives from daily incidents, which, for their own reasons, have appeared significant and which are incorporated into their play and talk until they are understood. Learning is the discovery of personal meaning. Each child organizes learning logically for himself, not just according to his intellectual abilities, but, perhaps more importantly, by the way his experiences are personally perceived. Working from this view, it is perhaps easier to understand how widely one child's knowledge and understanding of any experience may vary from another child's of the same age and intellectual capacity. So it seems to be also with the child's knowledge and understanding of death. Recent reviews of the topic (Essa & Murray, 1994; Speece & Brent, 1984) find the research literature to be ambiguous as to whether any direct link exists between a child's level of cognitive development and his or her conceptualization of death.

The research I have completed of children's perception and concept of death and the process by which their concepts are developed uses the four questions asked by Koocher (1973, 1974a, 1974b). However, it varies from all of the work reported so far in that I also used two play situations. I was interested in exploring further the idea that there is a gap between thought, action, and language in young children. The emphasis on normality aside, there is, of course, much to learn from the child who faces a more immediate death. What a child does or does not communicate about death should be viewed as indicative of what he chooses to reveal rather than any complete expression of thought on the matter (Bluebond-Langner, 1978). Precisely, what children can communicate may only be in non-adult terms and, therefore, may go unrecognized and untapped by paper-and-pencil measures (Sparta, 1987). Interestingly, it has been noted that children will choose with whom they communicate about death (Lansdown, 1989). In the case of a dying child, he will develop different modes of communication, all the while determining who can deal with his pain and who cannot (Orbach, 1988).

Most research has relied on question-and-answer techniques alone as a source of information on children's concepts. In contrast, Wenestam and Wass (1987) have found a qualitative approach to be useful in the study of children's concepts of death. Fisher and Fisher (1993) argue that the questionnaire method of measuring death anxiety faces serious limitations. Particularly in the period from the ages of about 6 to 8 years, when concepts seem to begin to come into focus more clearly, such paper-and-pencil techniques may not provide an adequate picture of what children are really thinking and feeling. Tasks such as play, which make fewer demands on verbal abilities, may meet with greater success in obtaining a more accurate view of how children conceptualize death (Speece & Brent, 1984). These alternative methods may allow for a more open exploration of children's feelings about death because children are exposed to fewer demands and situational and emotional pressures (Stambrook & Parker, 1987). Even adults who believe young children lack real knowledge of death will realize that children experience intense emotions when thinking of death (Vianello & Lucamante, 1988).

As Piaget (1951) was well aware, children often say things that may make adults think that they grasp a concept when in fact they are just quoting adults or reflecting the influence of other outside sources and do not, as yet, have the inner concept to match the words or phrases they dimly know are expected of them. Regardless of whether children hold some form of understanding about death, their limited language skills almost preclude any worthwhile assessment of such cognitions (Stambrook & Parker, 1987). By the same token, children may have thoughts and feelings that they are unable to articulate clearly, and thus they also cannot reveal to an adult the full extent of their understanding. Lazar and Torney-Purta (1991) echo this belief. Unfortunately their solution of teasing out from the established parameters (e.g. irreversibility) even smaller bits to study only recapitulates an already narrow cognitive view of the issue. By observing the child at play as well as listening to what he says in response to our questions, we may be able to compensate for this gap in communication. Play is the child's unique tool for exploring, understanding and shaping his world (Weininger, 1979b). By paying close attention to the ways in which the child plays out situations associated with death and dying we may be able to gain further insight into his concepts and feelings and possible relationships between them.

Sixty children took part in this study (Weininger, 1979a). They ranged in age from 4 to 9; they were all from one school, in a middle-class urban area, from intact families, and they were judged to be of normal intelligence. None of them had experienced either parental separations or parental deaths, and none had had any unusual emotional, physical, or academic problems. Each of the six age groups, composed of nine to twelve children, was made up of roughly half boys and half girls. The children were seen one at a time for approximately thirty minutes each in a classroom prepared with play materials, a tape recorder, and a small table and chairs. In the play procedure, the interviewer presented all the materials, consisting of mother-, father-, and child-dolls, a stethoscope, hypodermic needle, thermometer, candy pills, a play double-bed, a blanket, pillow, a box with a lid (coloured black and measuring 2" × 6" × 3" deep), paper and pencil, and a glass of water.

Each child was seen in two play situations presented in random order to the children. In one play situation, the child was told "The doll *is* very sick, and the doll is going to die." In the other play situation, the child was told, "The doll *was* very sick and is now *dead.*" Initially there was an attempt to make the child feel comfortable in the situation with the stranger before presenting the play situations. The interviewer gave the child time and, if necessary, helped to play out each situation, encouraging the child to play in a free fashion and to say what was happening as he played. The discussion part of each session consisted of a conversation including the four Koocher questions, asked directly and without elaboration. However, the child was encouraged to talk about his responses. If he declined to answer, the discussion was changed to a more general one. Interestingly, most of the children were eager to talk about their ideas of dying and being dead, and they elaborated on them in considerable detail.

Responses and actions of the 4-year-old children indicated that they did not usually understand the concept of dying and dead. They consistently answered that they did not know when asked, "What makes things die?" or "How do you make things come alive?" They did not seem to understand the permanence of death or, as one would expect, the distinction between animate and inanimate objects. The question of making things come alive does not really register because, for the child of 4, things have not died. In the play situations, children of this age consistently did not have the doll die. They always played in a rather frantic way, giving medicine, talking about father and mother, waking the dolly up, pushing the dolly around, and talking about all sorts of nice things that have happened at home. There were no words or logical concepts available to these 4-year-old children that they could use to describe what they were feeling.

On a conscious level, then, death does not seem to have any meaning for them. However, the anxiety of these children is seen in their play and seems to me to indicate some apprehension of death on an unconscious level. I consider the way in which they were playing to be a demonstration of their concern about the potential loss of their parents. The 4-year-olds talked about the doll parents as though the parent were either going to save them or really do something magical to prevent something bad— that is, death—from happening. I think that in talking about the parents as the people who should save the child from dying, the children were expressing the fear that the parent might be lost or not capable and strong enough to stop the dying, or perhaps might be angry with the child and actually allow the child to die. I am suggesting that their play demonstrated what was really their major concern. Essentially, then, the 4-year-olds do not understand consciously the concepts of dying and dead. No doll died, and if the child did say the doll died, none of the dolls remained dead. Their frantic efforts saved the doll. The parents saved the doll from dying. The parent proved to be the good integrated object and not a persecutory one.

Five-year-olds showed considerable contrast to the 4-year-olds. Unlike the 4-year-olds, they knew what makes you die and had very specific answers: arrows, bullets, and spiders make you die. For them, things come alive again through resorting to medicine and hospitals. The 5-year-olds showed a thinking level that seemed to become more concrete, and it certainly sounds from their answers as if they regarded death as a very reversible process and not a permanent state.

Interestingly, the 5-year-olds also showed a kind of reincarnation theory as an explanation of what happens after death—either that they would "Go to Jesus" or "Go to Heaven." While they were talking in a way that seems to suggest that they had some beginning concept of dying and dead, their play did not support this. At this time, children were saying one thing but playing out another. I think their words were repeated things they had heard, and their play demonstrated their non-acceptance of death. Perhaps they were repeating words they had heard but were playing what they actually felt. Their thinking seemed to be at a very operational level in that they did use specific means to inflict death, but their play was certainly indicative of a pre-operational level of thinking with an almost intense as well as frantic denial of death. Even after the play situation was set with a dead doll, these 5-year-olds consistently had the doll getting better. Fantasy and magical thinking still prevailed. Essentially, the 5-year-old may say one thing but do another. He does not as yet have a concept that embraces the terms "dying" or "dead"; perhaps his phantasy is that the parent would never let "me die". The denial of a bad internal object is still prevalent, and perhaps their ego is not mature enough to embrace this aspect of death because it is experienced as "badness" or even as retribution.

The 6-year-olds were really the know-it-alls. They talked as if they knew what death was all about, and their answers sounded very formal and abstract. They talked about being ill and about body organs stopping, but only one of the nine 6-year-old children said that there was no way you could make things come alive again. All the others indicated reversibility in such statements as, "God will make you come back" or "You have a baby that comes back" or "You can plant people, burying them, and then the ground brings them back to life." The 6-year-olds seemed to understand that when you die you are buried. Once again, however, in the play situation, they consistently did not have the doll die. Some of the 6-year-olds used needles and medicine and operations, and a few used mother and father to prevent death. When the play situation stated that the doll was dead, five of the children denied that the doll was dead, and the others moved the idea from death to sleep. Their play behaviour did not indicate that they had the understanding that their language seemed to indicate—that is, while their language seemed to indicate a formal operational thought process, their play did not. They could understand potential causes for death and seemed to have the idea that they were going to die, but this was very much at variance with the concept that they presented of the reversibility of death. Perhaps, here again, we see the gap between the cultural representations and verbalizations of death (perhaps as the result of television and their parents) and their real understanding of it. It is almost like the 2-year-old who can parrot the whole alphabet after exposure to "Sesame Street" but cannot recognize any one letter out of sequence, nor understand what the letters are used for. The 6-year-old seems to understand and talks in an understanding way, but the play behaviour does not entirely indicate this. These 6-year-olds do not appear to understand the concepts of dying and dead.

Seven-year-olds seemed to demonstrate an abstract idea of what makes things die. There was an abstract cluster of ideas dealing with old age and bodily deterioration, as well as diseases and specific means of unnatural death, such as falling off a cliff or having a brick drop on your head. But the 7-year-olds still did not recognize that dead people do not come alive again. If you take good care of the person by giving oxygen, air, and needles and use special machines, "he will come back again". Only three of the twelve children at the 7-year-old level seemed to doubt that dead people could be brought back to life, and eleven children said that the person would be buried when he died, but they did not seem to relate it to themselves, projecting it to others. When presented with the dying doll, in all cases they managed to get the doll better. When the doll was dead, eight of the 7-year-old children said it was buried, but four said that it got better and went home. The 7-year-olds still had some residual conflict about death. They seemed to understand what made things die, but they seemed to have difficulty with the concept of permanence. I think that this situation created much anxiety for them as was indicated by their not talking about themselves but talking about things outside themselves. I think their play demonstrated that they were attempting to integrate the concept of death but that they had not been able to do so as yet. The phantasy of death as retaliation was still present, and ways to save themselves were very important. These ways seem to indicate that the ego has matured to a position where a variety of controls over badness is possible. Bringing goodness and badness together does not necessarily mean badness "wins out".

Eight-year-olds were a little more precise in their answers, and by this age there were elaborate clusters as to death causes, such as lung cancer, blood circulation problems, heart disease, and being run over by an automobile. Surprisingly, only three of the ten talked about death as permanent. All ten 8-year-olds, in a play situation with the dead doll, talked of having a burial, going to Heaven, and being with God. In terms of their play, they demonstrated the concept of dead, but when asked about it there was some doubt. The concept was not fully integrated yet and, I suspect, had not as yet reached a formal thinking process. The child could play-act the dead scene accurately, but the language of some of the 8-year-olds indicated a difficulty with its verbal conceptualization. They played it out accurately, but they did not verbalize it accurately—in contrast, to the 5-year-olds, who played it out inaccurately but verbalized it fairly accurately.

Bright answers about causes of death were typical of the 9-year-olds. They recited a huge catalogue of causes, ranging from starvation, murder, and suicide to bodily deterioration. Generally, they felt that things could not come alive again, and they did not think that there was a cure for death. The 9-year-olds had a very clearly defined concept as to what would happen to them when they died—they would be buried and have a funeral.

In the play situation, they all buried the dead doll with no hesitation, indicating, I think, that the concept had been understood and integrated. By this age they demonstrated that they understood, both in play and in language, the concept of dying and dead.

Neither the words nor the actions of 4-year-olds and several 5-year-olds seemed to indicate an understanding of death. At 6 and 7, many children's facility with borrowed language makes it sound as if they understand causes for death, while their play still demonstrates a lack of understanding of the permanence of death. At 8, this shifts slightly; they can play it out accurately, and they now have enough cognitive and language skills to express some doubts verbally about the concept of death. Only at the age of 9 do play and words seem to fit together in an integrated way that includes universality and dying as part of an internal bodily process of ageing, as well as the result of specific causes and permanency.

I think this discrepancy at various ages between action and words is important to note. Since we have tended to base our work with children about death on what they have said about death, some insights provided by a recognition of the gap between language, feelings, actions, and thoughts may be useful in assessing how accurate our expectations of children are when they are exposed to death as well as in deciding how to talk with them most sensitively and intelligibly. I think that if we consider carefully the work on discovering what children understand about death, we can develop some useful ideas about more effective communication, both as parents helping children to assimilate their experiences meaningfully and as professionals dealing with dying children and grieving parents. It is difficult, perhaps impossible, to determine whether the reaction of children even as young as 1 year of age—to the death of a parent or a sibling, for example—is mourning in an adult sense or a much more severe form of the sense of loss, anxiety, and rage occasioned by separation from a parent not just for a brief time, but for ever. With this understanding that many children do not have an accurate concept of death as permanent and irreversible until they are nearly 9, it would be difficult to suggest that they are reacting with adult-like grief because of a sure knowledge of total and irrevocable loss through death. I think they are reacting to the loss of an introjected good object that is no longer available. Because the phantasy of an internal good and relieving object seems to need the presence of an external object that reinforces the sense of one's own internal goodness, the loss of that external object through death forces the internal introject to become bad. The phantasy of being able to relieve one's own tension and discomfort can only last for a certain amount of time in children, as well as in some adults. The child's ego requires the environment to support the phantasy, just as the baby's thumb can only relieve the sense of hunger tension for a while— the sense of relief must be supported by the nipple and nurturance. If not present, then the internal object begins to turn bad and is phantasized as a persecutor.

A dying child, as Spinetta (1974) indicates, may be aware that something very serious is happening to him. He may be aware of his own pain and also of the pain and sorrow that surrounds him as experienced by the anxiety and sadness of nurses, parents, friends, and physicians. However, without having attained a stage of cognitive development that includes a concept of death as permanent, it seems unrealistic to see children as going through the same terrible rage, sadness, and resignation cycle as do dying adults. It is, however, realistic to see children as experiencing the sense of persecution because their internal object has turned bad.

Much of the guilt, sorrow, and anxiety of parents faced with the death of a child is due not only to their accurate understanding of the permanency of death, but also because of their knowledge of the experiences and joys that their child will miss and, importantly, that they will miss sharing with him. Their feelings are also due to their strong frustration at not being able to "make it all better" for their child. In contrast, much of the rage of the young dying child is at the separation from, and the loss of, his parents because of hospitalization and also the knowledge that his parents could not work the magic he had thought they could. Kissing him did not "make it all better"— something that is really very hard for children, and perhaps even for adults, to accept. The introjected good object, as strengthened by the real parent, is now not a powerful object. If the external parent cannot help, then the strength of the goodness of the internal introject of the young child gradually diminishes. This, combined with the child's anxiety about the fear and sadness sensed in the parents, causes him to view himself somehow as the one to blame, the one who has brought on these feelings.

There is, I think, a projection of the child's own fears and sadness with subsequent anxiety of retaliation as well as ego depletion. This also reflects the child's very egocentric view of the world. This may further separate him from his family, just at the time he most needs to know the safety of their love and closeness. The child's sense of being able to be contained by his parents has been reduced. His sense of security and safety is greatly diminished because he experiences their pain as well as his own in himself and in them. The parents cannot seem to contain the child and give a sense of security. Their reactions to the child's impending death makes them "leaky containers". I suspect that much of the seeming callousness displayed by the personnel of institutions (which deal so effectively with medical but not always with emotional and psychological realities of dying children and their families) stems not only from frustration at not being able to save the child, but also from their inability to come to terms with this fact. Perhaps the young child's immature conceptual view of death contributes to this state as well.

We must clearly recognize that young children cannot understand that death is permanent, nor can they grasp what will happen to them. Thus, our concern in dealing with dying children or children exposed to the death of a parent or friend should be to help allay their anxiety at the actual or potential separation from a loved person. We must not try to project our grief feelings about the loss of future relationships onto the child, who can only comprehend this by an egocentric action or reaction in assuming he must have done something wrong. The adult's reaction to the finality of death will not be the same as that of the young child who does not understand what this means. It is not strange, then, for a young child, upon learning about the death of a parent, friend, or relative, to say, "When can we go and have hot dogs?" or "Can we watch television?" This is not an insensitivity on the part of the young child. It is, I think, a non-understanding about death as well as a sense of some "danger" coming from the person who is telling the child about the death. Young children pick up feelings from others and generally introject these feelings, which become part of the inner ego workings. When the potential introject is dangerous, like the feelings a child picks up about death, then most children will try to avoid the realization of these.

One 5-year-old girl I knew said that she knew her granddad "was dead, so let's go and have a hamburger." She was not "callous". She was, I think, not only unable to understand the meaning of death, but she also needed to avoid the feelings she was sensing from others. She needed nurturing to make sure her own sense of internal goodness was maintained.

We must also try to ascertain what the child's concrete concept of death is and encourage him to talk about it and perhaps, when possible, to play it out with the adult. If it is anxiety, fear, anger, or hostility that the child is feeling, we should try to recognize whether it is his concept of death or his reaction to the adults' feelings around him that is causing this reaction. In either case, it is important to allow the child the free expression of such feelings. Many play materials are available for such a purpose. Psychotherapy sessions with groups of children may also be helpful in increasing their understanding and in identifying areas of misunderstanding about what is happening to them or has happened to them when they have experienced the death of a parent or relative. The play allows them to integrate their feelings of reality and prevents the separation and split in thoughts and feelings that makes it extremely difficult for them to cope with the intellectual understanding of death and the phantasies about their internal objects. If their feelings as well as those of important others are not understood and experienced, then, I think, it is very difficult for these children to "re-invest" their emotional sense of safety and security in others who are willing to contain them.

We should not try to give children information that is confusing or inappropriate in terms of their understanding about death, no matter how comforting it is for us to do so. Explanations of death that imply reversibility or lifelike behaviour after burial may create considerable anxiety in the child who has just begun to understand death as permanent. The younger child may find burial very frightening if he has been led to believe that people wake up again afterwards. As a 4-year-old boy said, "How will Granny get out of the box after she wakes up? She'll be in a very dark place and she'll be frightened, won't she?" Providing children with a "sugar-coated" impression about how lovely Heaven is when they have lost a parent or are nearing death themselves is likely to create confusion if they try to reconcile this with the fear that they sense in the adults around them. If Heaven is such a great place, then why are the adults crying?

To try to force an understanding when the cognitive framework to do so is not yet there is, I think, futile. To try to make most 4-year-olds realize that death is forever is probably impossible, and it would certainly be anxiety-provoking and confusing to insist that the child verbalize this for the benefit of the adults' "peace of mind". The child will repeat this for an adult, but the cost to the child is too great. The child's ego is not prepared to adjust to such an understanding.

Perhaps these ideas give us some indications of pitfalls to avoid. It made it easier for me to know that many of the very young children with whom I worked who were dying or experiencing another's death did not really understand that death meant "forever and never again". It helped me to approach the discussion of death, either as an experience in the child's external world or as an impending personal experience, but always at the level of the child's understanding and ego level. Perhaps our willingness to approach children this way depends upon our own personal ability to accept dying as part of living and on our own philosophy about immortality. Within these very general guidelines, a few suggestions seem indicated. For example, before giving answers or causes, I gently try to discover what the child already thinks is happening and try to fit my explanation into words and ideas that will not be out of place in terms of the child's concept. I allow and encourage the expression of feelings in any way with which the child seems comfortable. I answer his questions as honestly as I can, not only within my own belief framework, but also with some incorporation of the family's belief system.

I cannot promise a dying child the certainty of life again or a different form of life after death, but I can assure him and only him in the following way: "The pain you feel now will stop and never be replaced by any pain, and when you die it will be very much like going to sleep, and when you are asleep, your parents and I will always think about you." I think that it is important to be honest about my feelings of sadness at the thought of not being together with the child to share things and at my sense of missing the child, as will the parents. I try to help the parents to understand and recognize the feelings that are bound up with the death by telling them what I will be talking about with their child and offering them the opportunity to be part of our talk. I think it is very important to reassure the child that there is nothing *he* said or did or felt that is to blame for this illness or disability or accident or for the adults' sorrow.

I accept an apparent lack of sadness on the young child's part as what may be a coping mechanism for handling his feelings and those of the parents. I think that this is also tied to a poorly understood concept. Anger may be expressed at the adults because they are not able to prevent or "take away" the pain. This anger may be shown by avoidance of the adults, as in, "I don't want to see you", or by not eating, or by screams and tantrums when with the adults. The anger is there because the internal object has turned "bad" and the once good introject is not able to overcome the pain. I think children see this as the result of their parents either not giving them something they need or taking back some of the goodness. In either situation, anger at the parents will be the result.

The parenting skills necessary to survive as the parents of a 2-year-old (acceptance of a variety of behaviours such as swings from dependence to independence, immature and regressive behaviour under stress, anger with no immediate apparent stimulus, separation anxiety, which brings on rage and tears, a sense of suddenly being lost and lonely, cuddling one moment and then suddenly refusing to be touched) are also the skills necessary to survive as a parent of a dying child, as a professional working with such a child, or as a parent of a child who has experienced the death of the other parent, or a sibling, or even a close playmate.

In the final analysis, we can only work through with another human being something we have come to terms with ourselves in the deepest recesses of our minds and hearts. Perhaps it is only through a personal knowledge that dying is as much a part of life as is being born, just as natural and as much an experience unique to each of us as an individual but universal to all of us, that the acceptance of it for ourselves and those we are most tied to—our children and parents—becomes possible. It really seems to be important for us to understand our personal knowledge about death. An anonymous Greek once said, "Physician, heal thyself!" Socrates stated, "Know thyself!" So, perhaps in order to really help our children to cope with death, we must first accept it in ourselves and then take some consolation from the knowledge that many children, at least, will be spared the awesome totality of its "forever and never again reality" as long as they are still young. They cannot think about it or understand it or talk about it as we do, but they do have very strong feelings, and it is these feelings that we must try to contain and gradually "return" to the children in an intellectual and emotionally understandable way.

CHAPTER TEN

Dying and disabled children
and children who feel unwanted

When Melanie Klein wrote about children and their phantasy life, to my knowledge there were no opportunities for her to observe and work with young children who were born with physically handicapping conditions. The developments of modern medicine have enabled many severely physically handicapped children to live—children who, I think, might have died just a few years ago. Now we have many vigorous methods to keep infants alive, and there are many documented cases of infants surviving for several years who have been able to compensate for and/or overcome many of their severe physical difficulties. However, the one aspect that has not been dealt with in these children is the "conscious support of circumstances conducive to healthy ego development. Consequently problems related to early emotional issues may be mis-identified or unintentionally exacerbated" (Saint-Cyr, 1994, p. 3).

I think that the immature ego of the infant is not capable of effective development, if not survival, under the continual stress of a severe physical disability (Weininger, 1975). Also, this stress makes it difficult to provide the necessary and sufficient conditions for the immature ego to differentiate itself from the external object—usually the mother. In such a case, a clear boundary between the baby's internal objects and the external objects cannot be effectively achieved, and the boundary remains within a fuzzy non-delineated state. The infantile ego and the external object are one and the same and remain so until the infant has been provided with sufficient good mothering experiences to enable the immature ego to develop and become strong enough to cope with the anxiety of aloneness, initially felt as discomfort and tension and then experienced as a sense of persecution.

Saint-Cyr (1994) clearly points out about the infant:

> In this state (non-differentiated boundary between ego and external reality) normal internal discomfort and frustration of his needs can be experienced with acute urgency and perceived as attacks by the part-object that is the bad breast, which Klein calls "the external representative of the death instinct". The consequent persecutory anxiety is experienced internally as an introjected bad object which heightens the sense of internal danger. As a defence against anxiety the infant will attempt to deflect this anxiety to the external world (the bad breast). [p. 2]

However, with excessive projection of internal bad objects, the immature ego remains in a weakened state and has difficulty taking in good experiences as they are experienced as becoming bad once internalized. The result becomes a refusal to take in anything, including foods, and survival is threatened.

The positive experiences of satisfaction would be experienced internally as an introjected good object and provide not only the opportunity for ego growth and strengthening, but also the re-inforcement of the life instinct. This is the desire to continue living, and even though anxieties may be part of living, there will be a sense that these anxieties can be dealt with and need not create a sense of annihilation—a sense of death.

As Klein pointed out, the continual introjection of good objects forms the nucleus around which the healthy ego will develop and become strengthened. The ego then acts in a way, as a cohesive centre, gathering the good-enough objects that enable the infant to master persecutory anxiety and cope effectively with the threat of disintegration and annihilation. As Klein suggested earlier and as Saint-Cyr (1994) goes on to explain: "The ability of the real external object, normally the mother, to accept and contain the infant's projected anxiety and to provide a sufficient degree of satisfaction, supports the life instinct, permitting the ego to deflect the sense of annihilation which threatens him" (pp. 2–3).

The infant who is born with a serious physical handicap may become overwhelmed in the struggle against the sense of psychological annihilation, even though the battle to prevent physical annihilation is successful. The physical discomfort is, I think, perceived as an internal attack, and the infant's attempt to preserve itself is to project the attack. However, there is little goodness that can be introjected when the physical state of discomfort and pain continues almost unabated for months, if not years. The constant projection must leave the ego in a continual weakened and fragmented state. Given the tenuous medical condition and the need for heroic medical and physical operations, the presence of a good-enough, containing mothering person seems unavailable, literally or emotionally, to help the infant to cope with the life-threatening physical state and the life-threatening emotional state. No one seems to be attending to the internal world of the baby—or at least that is the way I conceive the baby to respond—and the ego remains fragile, weakened, and susceptible to death, both physically and psychologically.

In the physical care of the baby, medical nutritive intervention must often substitute for the satisfaction of the nipple, and often we have found that when oral feeding is initiated, the immature ego is threatened by this feeding, which may mean tube feeding. Thus, feeding itself becomes a persecutory experience. For example, the baby's fingers may not be able to reach the mouth, or there may be no fingers, or the mouth may be malformed, which may trigger gagging, or the inserting tube may feel very uncomfortable.

Breathing may be a difficult experience; it may be laboured, and the baby may need a physical device for extended periods of time in order to breathe. In these cases, breathing itself may contribute to a sense of annihilation—it just becomes too painful to breathe—and the baby, I suspect, may interpret this as another bad threatening object.

We can see, then, how these babies have very limited opportunity to introject a good internal object. I think the on-going irritability, discomfort, and pain becomes experienced as terror of annihilation, which contributes to the persecution anxiety and, therefore, to the refusal to "take in" because taking-in (breath, for example) is painful.

In a letter, Lise Saint-Cyr describes a case that is, we think, related to the sense of annihilation experienced by an 8-month-old baby.*

You asked if I had any more examples related to the death instinct. During your course, your discussion of the death instinct stimulated fresh insights for me about this area. I am beginning to understand the potential impact of the early struggles with basic survival issues, and the fear of annihilation that these babies (and their mothers) have to cope with. Of course, they have more than the normal discomforts of infancy (e.g. repeated seizures, choking on feeds, frequent surgery). I can see that the infant's ability to rally can depend on the mother's capacity to contain and cope with the baby's projections. However, examples that come to mind are not clear-cut and are open to alternate interpretations, especially given the medical complications involved.

None-the-less I have used this perspective recently and was impressed with where it quickly led. I was asked to consult to a developmental therapist who wanted advice about a mother and an 8-month-old girl with developmental delay. The mother was Pakistani, the father was Arab, and the mother felt that the baby's welfare was entirely up to her. Recently the baby had become highly irritable, was waking frequently at night, and was beginning to gag and vomit when fed. She was not responding to remediation efforts, and there did not seem to be any physical cause. This was apparently a recurring phenomenon.

The therapist attached to the case described a progressively overwhelmed, depressed mother, who said that she felt as if the baby was "doing these things" to her on purpose. My impression was that the baby was projecting feelings of

---

*Personal communication, 13 June 1994. Permission to quote the letter was kindly given by Lise Saint-Cyr.

distress to a mother who was increasingly unable to contain and cope with the projections, which she interpreted as attacks. I felt that the baby, rather than identifying with a protective breast, was experiencing persecutory anxiety in response to the mother's distress. Her internal sense of danger was causing everything she tried to take in to turn bad, so that what little food she accepted was vomited. My sense was that her irritability might be a result of excessive projection that was resulting in a weakened, fragmented ego state. In that case her lack of response to remediation efforts might reflect an attempt to shut down altogether. It appeared that the mother felt helpless to protect her daughter from a sense of annihilation, and she felt she had few, if any resources left to minister to her baby; she felt as if she were falling to bits. I had the impression that the baby was losing the battle and the death instinct was gaining.

What I said was that I was concerned that the life force was draining away from them both as their relationship fell apart. I was startled (I think she was too!) when she then told me that during the worst of it, the mother had threatened to kill her baby and herself. One of the main concerns of the therapist (who is experienced in dealing with developmental problems) was that her interaction with this mother tended to leave her, as well, feeling hopeless and inadequate. Though the situation was currently stable, she was concerned about her capacity to quickly identify and deal with a recurrence of this crisis, and about what steps to take to head it off. My impression was that her feelings were a result of countertransference. By clarifying her own feelings and recognizing her own reactions to the overwhelmed mother, she was better able to understand the mother's feelings, and their interaction with those of the baby. As an occupational therapist, I would ordinarily have been expected to address specific issues such as the feeding problem, and the lack of developmental progress. Our discussion took a very different course, and my sense was that it was more pertinent to the therapist's real concerns.

Exactly one month has elapsed. In a follow-up conversation today, the therapist told me that the mother has begun to attend a parent support group. She now perceives her husband at least as *caring* about the baby though he is still not much practical help. She no longer feels that the baby is "doing these things to her" on purpose, and the therapist feels that she is starting to be able to "see things from the baby's point of view". The baby is doing more on her own and she is accepting a wider range of food without vomiting (though she is still very fussy about food). Unfortunately, it appears as though some hostility is spilling over to a 4-year-old sibling whom the therapist observed being pinched yesterday by the mother. Evidently this is a work in progress but at least the infant is eating and now progressing. The therapist will no doubt have to try and help mother with her feelings to both her babies.

This is not an exceptional example, although maybe more extreme than usual. I've often seen stressed relationships deteriorate because of escalating irritability affecting both the mother and infant, usually combined with a sense of inadequacy on the mother's part, and then a deterioration in the feeding process. Of course, many of these kids are often so close to the edge already that failure to thrive can be physically catastrophic. It is understandable that therapists feel compelled to rush in with any new technique they can think of to throw at the problem. Nevertheless I'm now convinced that the threat of annihilation needs to be addressed on an emotional level, especially in a case like this. One problem in the case I described is that I sense that the therapist will need on-going support to hang on to the concept, though that may be a bit of a projection of my own!"

An infant who, despite early physical trauma, succeeds in identifying with an ideal breast that is felt to be strong enough to protect him will be better able to cope with the continuing pain and phantasized hostility. If excessive projection of hostile bits of the ego can be counterbalanced by good-enough satisfying experiences with a containing mother, who will, I think, need support, then the ego will gradually become sufficiently integrated to differentiate itself from the external object and begin the hazardous journey to attempt to cope with anxieties. Bodily sensations will become more differentiated and increase in strength, enabling greater ego capacity and strength to cope with pain and to develop methods for ego relief. However, the depressive pain of fear of damage to the external object may become potentially a greater threat in an infant with handicaps than in one without handicaps. Reparation to the object seems impossible because it is difficult, or in some cases impossible, to gain ego resilience, strength, and a sense of goodness. This would be the case, for example, if the infant continues to be subjected to repeated or prolonged stress, resulting in a need to project a great deal of pain and hostility. If, in reality, oral, urethral, and anal sensations are consistent sources of pain, the baby will phantasize that food, urine, and faeces are dangerous to its internal world (if not to its real world) and attempt to rid itself of these frightening and painful sensations. Projection, however, increases the baby's phantasized destructive potential and increases the baby's fear of retaliatory aggression. Whether the primary object is eventually internalized as a good object or as a retaliating, persecutory object depends on the infant's confidence in his reparative efforts and on the mother's capacity to contain his, as well as her own, very painful feelings. How the mother contends with such problems can influence the infant's ability to cope with the fear that he has damaged the good object and to cope with his subsequent regression to greater persecutory anxiety.

Saint-Cyr (1994) presents the following case of a child with severe handicaps:

> Karen was an infant aged thirteen months whom I treated until age thirty-six months. Throughout this period, all of her primary body sensations were potentially persecutory. Repeated painful urinary tract infections would make their presence known by obvious blood in the urine (fever being too common in this child to be a reliable clue). Constipation was so severe, despite mother's attempts to prevent it, that she regularly had to be dis-impacted manually. She tended to choke on mucus, in which case she would need immediate suctioning to breathe, round the clock. Feeding frequently provoked gagging and choking. She was so sensitized to gagging and vomiting that it was decided to do a fundoplication to make it physically impossible for her to vomit, a frightening consequence in itself. The mother made effective and continued use of all her personal and professional resources to accept these challenges with relative equanimity and Karen progressed.

In this case, despite continued persecutory threats to the infant, the mother was able to cope well enough with the many complications to permit Karen to develop surprisingly well, despite her multiple handicaps. If such problems are not adequately contained, they seem to develop into a destructive, hostile interaction pattern with the mother.

Karen's development was compromised by seizures, and by visual, hearing, cognitive, and motor deficits (including very low muscle tone) secondary to cytomegalovirus inclusions disease in the first trimester. Currently, at age seven, Karen reportedly is a happy child who interacts warmly with her family (including one younger and one older sibling, who are also doing well). She differentiates among family and friends, uses a number of words meaningfully, and participates happily in a special educational program. Her family love and accept her, and have settled down to a relatively normal life. Her parents continue to be happily married. In retrospect, one of the interesting questions about this child is, "What went right?"

In addition to the encouragement of a loving husband and understanding grandparents, the mother also received considerable practical and professional support, which was carefully monitored and coordinated with both parents' active involvement. Karen and her mother were seen weekly, and sometimes twice per week, for about two hours each time. Sessions with me involved a combination of counselling and teaching and were video-taped by her. These tapes were viewed by either parent, but especially the mother, who reports that she often watched them over the course of several years, whenever she felt that she was "losing it". I interpret the mother's use of the videotapes in this way as an indication that they were fulfilling a "containment" function, in that the mother could see herself as functioning effectively at that time.

The focus of counselling was on resolution of the mother's (and sometimes father's) feelings of grief, and on family and sibling issues. The focus of the work with Karen, rather than being "milestone oriented," was on sensory-motor and feeding issues. Mother was consistently supported in her role and she, in turn, became quite expert at meeting Karen's needs. She attempted to respond promptly, particularly because, given Karen's significant vision and hearing deficits, her attempts to communicate her needs were felt to be especially significant. By responding promptly, Karen's phantasy of being able to be comforted was never thwarted. The emphasis on sensory input was similarly prompted by the inference that it was important for Karen to have a sense of her body's boundaries and of her position in space. Consequently, we focused on deep proprioceptive input through the head, trunk, and limbs, as well as proprioceptive work to sensitize her to where her centre of equilibrium and base of support were. Mother also did gentle infant massage, and gradually introduced her to varied sensory stimuli. I took care to announce my presence to her with a consistent physical and verbal signal and by always wearing the same one-of-a-kind perfume. Toward the end of my involvement with Karen she began to use a reasonable approximation of my name. She smiled and gurgled and appeared to be trying to cooperate as her mother and I worked, often with the mother's hands on the baby and my hands over hers as a guide. The mother always prepared the same textured blanket for us all to sit on together, and which she used only for this purpose. The mother was able to provide a caring, consistently loving setting for her baby. This no doubt allowed the baby to project her fears and angers to her mother, but also gave her mother a sense of providing a consistent and loving atmosphere and environment which took in the baby's feelings and did not give the baby a retaliatory feeling. The phantasy of retaliation was countered by the safe world that the mother created. Reality altered phantasy and the ego not only survived but flourished. [Saint-Cyr, 1994, pp. 12–13]

We do not have words from babies and toddlers but we do from older children who have experienced great pain, and when they talk about death and dying, their pain is so clear. They have been left alone, they feel lost, they are not contained, and they have little to counter the persecution and great discomfort they feel daily. There is no one there to hold them and to support the ego that is so frequently just about ready to disintegrate.

Some powerful phrases from children were reported by Valerie Yule (1979). Damian, a mildly retarded, hyperactive 7-year-old child, wrote upon failing at school:

Reality	Dream
Name's John	*our car*
He fall—hard	*cars go faster*
hit a wall	*going to crash*
hit the bricks	*crash in the post*
hit a fence	*boat comes along*
hit bike	*car gets crash*
go faster	*boat goes on the water*
it break	*boat crash*
bump head	*car crash in the boat*
	car turn around
	car goes on the road
	crashes
	car
	crashes

[Yule, 1979, p. 74]

And so Damian, in both his real world and his dream world, only experiences pain. Speed is important to him and always results in a disaster—being annihilated. It is as if Damian could try to work hard at school, but all he would experience would be the hyperactive speed of his own being and the pain of his failed attempts. His sense of failing and not being is expressed by his crashing—a sense of utter helplessness.

Sergie, a very aggressive 9-year-old boy, who felt that "everything" was against him and no one cared for him, wrote:

> That person is going to his friend's place and—then he had to go to a different place—and he got lost in the town—and then when some people come they—thought he was a bird—then they come with a gun and killed that boy—and the policeman came and told him which one—did he kill—and he said, "I killed a bird"—and the policeman came around there he found the—dead boy. He collect his mother, a few days [later] he was dead. [Yule, 1979, p. 76]

Sergie's attempts to find friendship quickly change to finding death. It is almost as if Sergie's sense of dependency is so unacceptable that he gets lost in a town where he is mistaken for a bird—perhaps a being that could escape a painful world. However, he is killed. But a policeman, a representation of the internal superego, appears, questioning the boy who admits to a killing he did not do, but for which he dies. Even his mother cannot help him. I wonder whether Sergie feels angry, a feeling that he cannot contain, and he looks for a friend, a mother, to help him, but they cannot contain his anger. In his confused and anxious state he says he killed a bird—or killed himself. Neither the bird nor he can escape. The anger can only be controlled by not being, by his annihilation.

Sharlene, an 8-year-old girl whose parents did not want her, was moved from one household to another. She says in a matter-of-fact way that nobody wants her, so she always keeps everything in a suitcase for when she has to go away again. She writes:

> The donkey was standing, for someone was . . .
> He had dropped someone else, they had dropped him
>   because they didn't like him
> and he was looking for someone else—sadly.
> And he didn't find someone, and he walked a bit,
>   and a little boy came, and he smiled at the little donkey,
>   and he said, "Did you buck him off or something?"
> and he nodded his head like that, as horses do,
> and he got on him and rode him around,
> and took him back to his owner—
> he took him back home and his mother said,
> "Take him away,
> take everything off him and take him away",
> —because they didn't like the colour of it,
> and they burnt it up because they didn't like it,
> and that was the end of the story,
> the donkey died
> got killed by a hunter,
> the pony walked away sadly and got killed by a hunter.

[Yule, 1979. p. 76]

No one wants the donkey, no one likes the donkey, and even when the boy tries to return him to his mother, she refuses to take him. Both the donkey and the pony are killed, no one seems to have survived. Sharlene is writing about herself and the pain of her sadness at not being wanted. I think all she is able to see in her future is not being.

CHAPTER ELEVEN

A three-year-old tries to understand death

T hree- and 4-year-olds are aware of death, and their ways of describing death often indicate the confusion they experience. They do try to organize their thoughts and their feelings, often not successfully, and often they are not able to pursue their feelings and ideas. These are just too painful.

Suzannah is a normal little girl, 3 years, 8 months of age, playing with Brian, an adult who is trying to understand the changes that normal children go through when they are offered a series of play sessions using art materials with an adult. Kendal, whom she mentions, is a friend who lives across the street and whose father had died before they moved to the neighbourhood. The following dialogue about dying and death was recorded during their twelfth session:

BRIAN: So you were telling me that Kendal's Dad is dead. Did he die just recently?

SUZZANAH: Yah, he just died recently.

Permission to quote part of this session was kindly given by Brian Nichols.

BRIAN: Just before they moved here.

SUZZANAH: Yah, he died . . .

BRIAN: So, you said to be dead means that you lie down and you can't move.

SUZZANAH: No . . . you're flat.

BRIAN: You're flat.

SUZZANAH: And your eyes are closed.

BRIAN: Uh hmm.

SUZZANAH: And never can open them. And you're gone forever.

BRIAN: Forever. So what other things can't you do when you're dead that you can do when you're alive?

SUZZANAH: You can't . . . you can't . . . umm . . . point your finger or move it or you can't move your toes.

BRIAN: Couldn't move them . . . no.

SUZZANAH: But you couldn't move your legs. The only thing that could move is your energy, but . . . not your whole body . . . just the energy of you.

BRIAN: Hmm.

SUZZANAH: That can just move . . . move.

BRIAN: Where can it move to? . . . the energy?

SUZZANAH: [using markers] Well . . .

BRIAN: So the energy . . .

SUZZANAH: Yup.

BRIAN: I'm not sure if I understand about the energy part.

SUZZANAH: Well, the energy is inside you . . . inside your bones . . . it's inside your bones.

BRIAN: Yup.

SUZZANAH: Like feel your bones in your knee. [Touches her knee]

BRIAN: [I touch my knee] Uh hmm. Yup . . . bones in my leg. [I touch my leg]

SUZZANAH: Like . . . how you die is you never [. . . *pause* . . .] can . . . umm . . . walk.

BRIAN: Uh hmm.

SUZZANAH: That your . . . that your energy can't move. But I know all about people dying.

BRIAN: How do you know about people dying? How did you find out?

SUZZANAH: Well, because one time my grandpa died.

BRIAN: Uh hmm.

SUZZANAH: And he was really flat you know. He was just like normal.

BRIAN: He was really flat.

SUZZANAH: Yah.

BRIAN: Did you see him in a coffin?

SUZZANAH: What?

BRIAN: Did you see him in a box . . . in a coffin? When you said he was flat.

SUZZANAH: Yup, he was in a coffin.

BRIAN: In a coffin.

SUZZANAH: One time he got hit by a car and he was flat.

BRIAN: Oh, I see. That's why he was flat . . . he got hit by a car.

SUZZANAH: Oh no. Oh no. He ate something. He got into a fight with a . . . got into a fight with a . . . a skunk and he got sprayed and then he went [*S. falls down*] but his energy can move [. . . *pause* . . .] like he died right now and . . . [. . . *long pause while she draws*]

BRIAN: So, when you said he died right now, is he dead forever or will he come back alive again?

SUZZANAH: He'll come back live again I'm sure. I'm sure he will.

BRIAN: When?

SUZZANAH: But now he's in a box. Like what you said.

BRIAN: Uh hmm. Yah, in a coffin—in a box.

SUZZANAH: No, he's not died now—he's alive now.

BRIAN: Where is he?

SUZZANAH: Well, he's in a . . . hospital . . . because he's a little too sick—so he's in a hospital cause his tummy . . .

BRIAN: Uh hmm.

SUZANNAH: . . . is really old and he'd feel like he's going to barf, so he went to the doctor's.

BRIAN: When you're not feeling well you barf, don't you.

SUZANNAH: But I barf at home but my grandpa barfs in the hospital cause of at home . . . the. Does that hurt?

BRIAN: Huh hum . . .

SUZANNAH: (*long pause*) Cause he . . . um . . . doesn't . . . um . . . know that . . . um . . . one time I got in . . . now I'm alive. One time I was died. But how I was died? I was on my side like this (*demonstrates*) a little on my side like.

BRIAN: So, just lying on your side and you were dead?

SUZANNAH: Ya. Not lying on my back That's usually how people die

BRIAN: On their sides?

SUZANNAH: Ya.

BRIAN: Right. Well, I didn't know that if you were dead you could come back again.

SUZANNAH: Well . . . you do that and if you don't come . . . sometimes you don't come. Sometimes you're dead forever.

BRIAN: Huh hum.

SUZANNAH: I don't care. I died dead forever . . . because I pretty old but not too old.

BRIAN: You had your birthday so you're not.

SUZANNAH: Four.

BRIAN: Four . . . four is pretty old.

SUZANNAH: No . . . old means that you're old in your head (*pause*) cause I don't know why people do that.

BRIAN: Do what?

SUZANNAH: One time I got hit by a car.

BRIAN: Did you?

SUZANNAH: But . . . I didn't get dead forever because now I am alive.

BRIAN: M . . . m . . . m . . . m. Well, some people can be hit by a car and not die. They can just maybe get a broken arm or get . . . or maybe a cut face.

SUZANNAH: Oh ya.

BRIAN: And other people might get hit by a car and could be dead forever.

SUZANNAH: Well . . . I just broke my arm when I got dead but I can still walk.

BRIAN: Huh hum.

SUZANNAH: And I can run and jump . . . I know. I wasn't dead. I just had a broken arm and then I went to the hospital and got really hard thick ousie. (*Points to her arm*)

BRIAN: So, you had a cast put on it.

SUZZANAH: Yah.

BRIAN: Was it white? [*Suzannah is using the white crayon*]

SUZZANAH: No—it was purple—I think.

BRIAN: Hum.

SUZZANAH: [*draws*] Like casts are purple and some casts are . . . no my cast was blue . . .

BRIAN: So, when you think about death, are there any pictures that you make, that are sort of about death?

SUZZANAH: Well, this one is about death.

BRIAN: Is it? Are those hearts?

SUZZANAH: Well, there's a nose, and he's died. I'm going to make some like there. He's like—on his side . . . [*talks about having her cast "clipped off"*] I know that if you die you're really flat and if you get died sometime, you'll see if you get a broken arm and maybe you'll get a blue cast if you go to my hospital cause they have tons of bandages. They have different colours. They have red, blue . . .

BRIAN: Wow. Almost anything.

SUZZANAH: And all these colours too. [*Touches box of markers*]

BRIAN: When you were hit with the car and had your cast, did you—were you flat?

SUZZANAH: No . . . no . . . no . . . no. I could still walk.

BRIAN: Okay. So flat means not being able to walk.

SUZZANAH: You're just lying.

BRIAN: What else can't you do when you're flat?

SUZZANAH: Well . . .

BRIAN: Can you talk?

SUZZANAH: No way.

BRIAN: No? Eat?

SUZZANAH: No.

BRIAN: Can you smell roses?

SUZZANAH: Well, you can still smell roses.

BRIAN: Still smell. Okay. Could you feel if I pinched you? Could you feel it?

SUZZANAH: Nope. [*Shakes her head*]

BRIAN: What if I sneezed on you?

SUZZANAH: [*laughs*] I'd be all gross. [*Laughs and then a pause . . .*] Like . . . like my cast was purple.

BRIAN: Not blue?

SUZZANAII: No. Purple. This dark. [*Shows colour with marker*]
. . .

[*During more than ten minutes of talking about death, Suzannah has made seven tiny shapes using six different colours of markers.*]

SUZZANAH: I'm going to draw a line that you can never ever go by. Markers are going to die if they go on that road. . . . [*Draws a vertical line down the middle of the paper*] This game is only for this four-year-olds because grown-ups will get died.

BRIAN: It's good to know that. I don't think I'm ready yet to die. I'd like to stay living still for a while.

SUZZANAH: But sometimes you fall and you do if you fall on your bum. Then never mind because you're not dead.

BRIAN: Umm . . . How did your friend's father die? Was he in a car accident?

SUZZANAH: Well . . . well, what happened . . . this is quite a big story.

BRIAN: Is it? Do you want to tell me or do you want to not tell me?

SUZZANAH: I want to tell you. They got into a fight, Dad and this skunk, and he died and the car ran over him and he died and . . . he didn't come back and . . . and he . . . umm . . . his energy, I mean . . . umm . . . moved and [. . . *pause* . . .] then when he got into a fight with the skunk he fell to the ground and he hit his head and then his whole body was . . . his bones was wrecked . . . his bones was bent like this [*shows me*]. That is how he was died.

At this point in the story, the telephone rings. and I leave the room to answer it. While I am away, Suzannah adds a long vertical green line to the centre of her picture. As I return, she immediately begins talking.

SUZZANAH: But he didn't die. I forgot. No, what I did . . . I didn't die but . . . umm . . . just the Dad died.

BRIAN: [*I sit down on the floor*] Yes, your friend's Dad died.

SUZZANAH: But the Mum didn't die of course then.

Brian was told later by Suzannah's parents that both of her grandfathers had died before she was born and that she has never had a broken bone or a cast, nor been in hospital.

* * *

Elenor, who is about to turn 4, said: "Mummy when you get dead, you will come alive again. Going away is like being dead because you're going away for a long time."

Perhaps it is only the internal phantasy of a good-enough mother that can save us, a good internal object that helps us cope with the anxieties of anger and retaliation. Children do try to make sense of separation, but to children separations are like death because there is no containing good-enough object for them. They sense potential disaster of being lonely and lost, perhaps because their egos are not strong enough to cope with their sense of retaliation from the departing object, which is gone and with which they are very angry.

I am grateful for the opportunity to play with young children and to talk with them about their ideas of death and dying. This work occurred because of my concern about children and their developing ideas about death, as well as, I think, our lack of knowledge about how children think about this very difficult experience.

CHAPTER TWELVE

Hospital and parental roles: deflection of the death instinct

T he most callous adult would not suggest that a disabled or dying child should be deprived of medication or treatment that would ease the pain of his living or dying. Yet, in many hospitals, children who have disabilities such as cerebral palsy, spinal bifida, or cancer are suffering needless emotional pain because it is so hard for each of us as adults to come to terms with physical handicaps and death, especially where children are involved. We often let our own feelings of dismay, grief, helplessness, sadness, bitterness, anger, frustration or impotence prevent us from adequately providing the psychological "medicine" that is so clearly essential for the comfort of these children.

I would like to make some observations about children's responses to physical illness and death and about some of the psychological factors involved in the emotional well-being of disabled and dying children and their families. I would like to illustrate the value of psychotherapy with these children and the effect it has on them, their families, and the hospital staff. It is my strong feeling that this help is as essential as any medical or physical treatment they receive. But changes need to happen in many hospitals if it is to be provided for them.

While working in hospitals, I found that children who are handicapped tend to perceive themselves as having unique disabilities, which, as many such children have said, have caused great trouble and disappointment to their parents. They imagine that their parents have put them in hospital because they want to get them out of their sight. This is probably the beginnings of a conscious breach in the relational assumption between parent and child. The parent faces the very difficult reality of the loss of valued achievement imagery—that is, the production of something that will last and give pleasure, as a source of personal potency—while the child experiences the loss of protection and safety. Such a child sees himself very negatively; he has little control over his body, little ability to tend to his own bodily needs, and much anxiety about himself as a reaction to the alienation he feels from his body and sometimes even from his parent. His body image is distorted, he feels vulnerable because of his loss of functioning, and he has a strong desire to hide his disability, if possible, in order to avoid identification with others like himself. Fisher and Fisher (1993) identify this issue as a "collective mastering of illusions to camouflage the reality of dying" (p. 42). Adolescents with cerebral palsy or muscular dystrophy can be seen to maximize a "nobody" cognitive dimension of their self-image, thereby trying to exclude as much of their somatic difficulty as they can (Fisher & Fisher, 1993). They tend to identify with very exhilarating non-self events and involvements that are external/outside themselves, such as sports, music, video and computer games, and fantasy role-playing games. Their aim, it seems, is to blunt the awareness of their bodies as a component of their self-identity. Severely handicapped children will often refuse to join organizations specifically set up for their disability because of their strong desire to see themselves as normal; they will also talk about funny mannerisms that people with disabilities have and about their own lack of any need to belong to such a group.

An interesting study on haemophilia by Goldy and Katz (1963) indicated that many haemophiliacs learn very early in life to hide their illness because of their awareness of people's feelings about how they should be handled. Concealment began in childhood in an effort to gain acceptance and was then carried on into adulthood to avoid being rejected by potential friends, employers, and even family. Goldy and Katz feel that the problems of the haemophilic are not greatly different from those faced by other chronically ill people who look normal.

It is when the child does not look normal that his relationships become difficult, if not impaired, perhaps as much by his own needs for concealment and a difference in his control over emotional reactions as by the responses of others, both imagined and real, to his appearance. This masking may also be the child's attempt to have the adults continue with their nurturing and administering of treatment (Sparta, 1987). In my conversations with young children and children aged between 10 and 14 years, they have often said that adults get "tired of them", and they say that unless they "pretend" and look like they're "fine" and respond in a "happy way", the adult does not pay as much attention to them and the adult gets "crabby". Children wear a mask to try to maintain adults' interest and concern, but so frequently it is at the expense of denying their emotions, hiding their fears, and, I think, of suffering even more pain. Young children with obvious disabilities often respond to others with overt withdrawal or, if pushed, with rage and anger. Their language is often a mirror of their feelings, from the direct, "Leave me alone!" and "I have got to go and be by myself", to "I need time to think about this alone." Children who look normal do not say these things as frequently; rather, they seem to say, "I will do it my way and bring it to you when it is finished . . ."—the implication being, "Don't look at what I am doing—don't watch me."

This denial of one's own illness is often accompanied by a child's belief in the control over his body being in the hands of some superior being, like a God—a belief often derived from the parents' inability to cope with the illness. The child may ascribe to this superior being a kind of magical control, which he may periodically either try to take from the superior being by a kind of acting-out behaviour or, through rituals and/or prayer, try to appease the superior being into being benevolent. When neither of these work, the child becomes even more anxious and/or angry because there seems to be no one to help. He must be so bad that God has forgotten and the parents do not help—they cannot make the pain go away. On the one hand, the child does not want not to be ill, nor to have to accept the disability or be identified by it to others; on the other hand, he needs the dependence on a superior being and the over-protection this should provide. This latter dependence often leads to a lack of ability to recognize danger in a situation and to cope with various aspects of reality in order to make effective decisions—that is, the child feels that he really does not have to worry because he is being taken care of and protected by this superior being. For example, one adolescent wheeled himself out of the hospital in his wheelchair to an area of the city where he could get illegal drugs. He crossed several very busy streets to reach the drug contact and then indiscriminately took what he was sold and ingested it on the spot. He said that he knew it was dangerous and that he should not do this because of the possible reaction of the illegal drugs he was sold with those prescribed for him as part of his treatment. However, he concluded by saying that he knew that nothing would happen to him: "I just know"! In therapy, I learned that he felt something was protecting him and that he did not have to decide whether something was good or bad because he would always be under this magical cloak. He would always be protected, not by his "parents" but by something he knew he could count on, and, as he then said, "It's something bigger than you or I and larger than my parents."

The child's denial of the reality of his own disability and his feelings of alienation often operate to create a gulf between him and his family. The child often talks about his parents as people who were unable to care for him and who probably did their best by sending him to hospital, but rarely does he talk about their feelings as sadness. Rather, he focuses on the disappointment he must be to them, the trouble and expense and worry he has caused, and the disruption for the rest of the family. The child's feelings of guilt are often made more acute by the parent's reactions to their own sense of helplessness when their child is further confronted with a secondary acute illness or further physical impairment. Often the parents feel even a stronger sense of guilt and impotence, wondering what they could have done to prevent the problems or what they should have noticed in order to report the possibility of further physical reactions. The further frustration in the face of such deterioration is felt by the child as a turning away and even as anger. The parents cannot make it "all better", and both child and parents know this. Unfortunately, little effort is made to address our mortality (Klatt, 1991). Parents may try to cope with their unvoiced anger by engaging many specialists and/or seeking many consultations, or by buying things for the child even if this causes a financial hardship for other family members. Their discomfort with their undealt-with anger results in shorter—and, as I found out, less frequent—visits. These visits may be marked by anger or irritation and by forays out of the room to look for something or buy something for the child in an attempt to deny their anger or guilt. In a similar pattern, Papadatou (1991) describes how the medical staff are often out of touch with their feelings about death and how this produces interpersonal tension. Here, again, the conflict is dealt with by wholesale denial in the form of pseudo-reparations (e.g. parties, get-togethers, gifts) at the service of maintaining these working.

In addition to these surface disruptions, the child's disability can often serve as a severe psychological disruption to family adjustment. I have seen a number of families that appeared intact at the time of the child's entry into the hospital, only to become fragmented and finally disintegrate, with the parents separating and, in some cases, other children in the family being sent to foster homes. Robert Noland (1971) has indicated that most parents experience their children's serious illnesses as very troublesome and ego-threatening. The children in these families reflect the emotional and social adjustment that their parents make, just as normal children in families do. We see the increased severity of this kind of identificational relationship when the child is severely disabled, for it is now the parents' sense of success and failure in helping their child that come into play. If the parents feel that they have done a fairly good job with their child, then the feelings of guilt and anxiety, coupled with rage, are lessened. In parents who have doubts about this kind of a relationship with their child, even relatively minor handicaps become catastrophic; the parents cannot endure the strain on their own psychological security, and they may have to separate to avoid the questioning eyes of their husband or wife.

Research, as reviewed by Stambrook and Parker (1987), reports how hospitalization factors such as the change in family relationships impact on how the child deals with the awareness of his impending death. The children have even greater distorted views of themselves. Their already shaky feelings of self-worth, of being loved and cared for, are called into question, and they respond with fear, guilt, inhibition, and anxiety, which also causes them to respond poorly in their interpersonal relations in hospital. Their physical disabilities and handicaps become expressed, not only by their body, but also by their psychological set.

A study by Galdston and Gamble (1969) noted that families of disabled children were very prone to displace affect and to become very emotional about issues not related to the illness, or else they tended to display feelings only through over-concern with such hospital routines as pulse-taking, checking, and recording. They also noticed that if the medical attitude was one of optimistic activity, the parents' attitude became more optimistic too. The implication for me here is that the parents not only are looking for solace in an authority, but they are exceptionally sensitive to anything coming from the physician or other hospital staff. Sometimes, in fact, I have noticed that parents have asked their children to smile when the doctor comes into the room—trying, I think, to have him say something encouraging so that they can be comforted and, in turn, can comfort their child. The parents in these situations need as much containing as do their children. In a small study I conducted at a hospital for physically disabled children, I noted that when the weekends came, the children who were anticipating a home visit became very anxious and irritable. They urinated more, their blood-pressure went up, and their sleep was fitful. If the home visit was cancelled because of a possible impending deterioration in their medical condition, the problems abated. It seemed that the children were reacting to leaving what they had begun to see as a "containing environment". The hospital as a structure became their "container", and they could not view themselves as "safe" at home. As one child said, "What happens if my mother freaks if I have a seizure?" These parents have lost their containing capacity, at least in the eyes of their children. The parents also need a container at this time, and with a container—perhaps a support group—their children would not view them as "leaky" (Weininger, 1972). The child and the parents need a person who is able to provide them with a sense of security in order to think through their difficulties and problems.

Professionals in hospitals often overlook how such factors as the child's feelings about himself and his illness and his relationships with his parents affect his response to hospital treatment (Stambrook & Parker, 1987; Vianello & Lucamante, 1988). If a child has multiple handicaps and is not responding to prescribed medication, he may be admonished by the physician for "not cooperating" and "not giving the medicine a chance to work". This is really a denial of the basic factors involved in the child's emotional make-up and in his response to physical illness. Children who are close to death quite correctly perceive the seriousness of a diagnosis and are more in touch with the reality of their approaching death than adults believe (Lanzi, Balottin, Borgatti, & Ottolini, 1993). If the child's situation is emotionally satisfying or gratifying, his response to the medication, as well as to physical forms of treatment, will be much more effective. If the level of anxiety that young children feel about the state of their bodies can be reduced, their ability to "take in" the medicine seems to improve; it is almost as if the incorporation is being prevented bodily because the child's whole bodily operation is already occupied by her or his anxieties (Weininger, 1989).

For example, I had the opportunity to observe a young baby of 3 months with a serious condition of osteogenesis imperfecta. For the first week, he cried fitfully, had difficulty sleeping, and seemed to be unable to respond to his caregivers and to accept his medications. The child was comforted by one nurse, who took into account the ease with which his bones cracked, stroked him gently while he lay in his cot, and talked to him, telling him how "careful" she would be with him and how she "liked to touch" him. Three nurses were assigned to be his caregivers, so that a familiar person was always there, no matter what the time, the shift, or the day. The boy developed a secure relationship with these people, and I think that for him, they represented not only his safety but also his beginnings of understanding—they talked about what they thought he might be worried about. Of course they were never "sure", but they tried to imagine how and what they might feel in his position, if that is possible. Their work and their relationship with him was very positive (Weininger, 1971).

His deterioration, both physically and emotionally, seemed to be arrested (although this was not expected), and the medication seemed to "take effect". Some might suggest that he became familiar with hospital routine, and this helped him. Perhaps so, but I think that it was the attachment he was able to form to his caregivers that gave him the needed security and safety to continue living. From my work with children living in hospitals, I have found that familiarity with routine does not lead so much to acceptance of medicine and treatment as it does to withdrawal, apathy, isolation, and, on occasion, acting-out behaviour. Even very young children of 5 and 6 can—and do—hide pills, drop them down toilets, stuff them into their ears and up their anus, or pass them out to other children.

Psychoanalytic psychotherapy with disabled children and their families can help to minimize anxiety, to work through guilt, and to allow the child and his parents to be able to respond to each other's sadness without guilt and anger. The child's medical treatment has a much better chance to work to greatest advantage when the child can begin to understand why he is concerned, guilty, angry, and anxious, and what his loss of function means—whether it be a loss of part of his body, a vulnerability that cannot be changed, or a sense of being so different from others. Psychoanalytic psychotherapy for the family may often be of major importance in providing them with the strength and insight into their own feelings and needs, which, in turn, enables them to provide a cushion of loving security and an atmosphere of open acceptance for the child. When they are able to recognize their own anger as futility and helplessness, along with disappointment and grief for the child or their personal inadequacy as parents and protectors, they are more likely to be able to deal in effective ways with their feelings and with the child. This effectiveness serves to alleviate the child's guilt and anxiety and, in turn, promotes the sense of emotional acceptance necessary to allow treatment to be as successful as possible. Effective psychotherapy may not only prevent serious disruption within the family but may also have an impact on the child's actual illness.

When death is imminent or inevitable, the feelings of children and their families are even more complex, although they have many of the same roots: guilt, anxiety, and anger over things undone or undoable. A study done by Friedman, Chodoff, Mason, and Hamburg (1963) indicates that parents usually have a feeling of hope when the child is first hospitalized, and then anger sets in when they understand that there is a limitation to medical assistance, that the miracles of modern medicine about which they have always heard so much will not be enough to save the life of their own child. The dying child often frightens us because the young child is often seen as a symbol of life, and we can offer very little justification for a child's death. Hope becomes limited, and the child becomes the symbol of his parent's own death anxiety (van Eys, 1987). Parents progress to self-blame for not having seen earlier manifestations of the disease, or perhaps for being inadvertent carriers of the genes or the tendency towards the illness. They feel guilty about things they have not done for the child, about occasions when they have not had time to spend with the child, or about times they were angry with the child. They may then try to compensate by over-indulging and over-protecting the child. But often the young child who is dying openly rejects his parents. He senses a kind of dependency on medical and nursing staff and hospital routines, yet seems to be afraid to show anger towards them in a direct way. Instead, this anger is directed at his parents, at whom he may also feel angry for not providing him with the total protection (i.e. breach of relational assumption) that young children unconsciously, if not consciously, expect from their parents. The child turns to the medical staff and holds on tight, with a lingering hope that these grown-ups will be able to provide the magic the child feels the parents are unable to provide.

Another study by Richards and Waisman (1955) on children dying of malignant disease indicates that as the child experiences a lowering of his own feelings of energy, he also experiences increased anxiety. The child seems to have difficulty talking about his impending death and suppresses his feelings about it. The child's reaction is a kind of passive acceptance—a resignation and depression that increases as the disease progresses.

In my experience, the most prominent emotion displayed by children who are dying of various diseases was anger. In the hospital the young child of 2 to 5 years of age quickly learned to be dependent on hospital staff and experienced great separation anxiety lest they leave him, as his parents did. This was followed by resultant resentment towards the staff as well as his parents. The child seemed to feel that he had failed and/or been failed by his parents and was then rebellious (though usually not verbally). Anger would take on the form of crying loudly when the mother was holding him, for instance. The slightly older child often talked in a way that might lead adults to think that the child understood what was happening to himself—that is, the child intellectualized his own death. A common theme was the child's feeling that he was being punished for some bad thoughts or actions. In therapy sessions such children expressed a great sense of guilt, and when the child felt the sessions were not helping him with this strong sense of guilt, he was quick to say, "I think I am no good and I won't try to live any more." If the therapy sessions were going along effectively and we were able to deal with the child's anxiety and punishment fantasies, then the child was no longer passively resistant but more openly rebellious, expressing considerable antagonism towards the hospital. At the same time, the child's desire for life and "will" to live was stronger. No longer did he "mope around" or talk about dying to the nurses. Now the child talked about doing things, wanted to visit places and said that he felt like eating.

The child of perhaps 6 or 7 would speak to me about death by expressing his fear in a confused and very angry way, still perceiving death as a punishment for being "bad". By this age, children seem to think that in some way they have caused their own illness and deserve to die. When I worked with these children in groups, the members of the groups were able to help each other with their feelings about their illness and dying. It usually took about five sessions before we were even able to say the word "death", and I recognized that we were about to use it when the children started talking about God, religion, and guilt. The sessions with the children (and at times their parents were invited to attend) helped them to cope with their sense of frustration and anger and relieved some of the anxiety about the future. These sessions also made it possible for children and parents to share the distress they were both experiencing but had not known how to voice, and to grieve for each other's loss and the future they would not have a chance to share. As van Eys (1987) aptly states, "the basic crisis of annihilation is not met with knowledge . . . but with character" (p. 121).

My experiences in hospitals with children who were physically handicapped and children who were dying taught me a great deal. One of the things I learned very early and very clearly was how to recognize my own feelings and how intricately bound up those feelings were with what I could do for the child. If I had to deny my own anger at their impending very early death, then I found that I was of no help to these children, that in fact the denial of my feelings only increased their sense of being "bad" and then their expression of "deserving to be punished". If I did not cope with my very sad feelings, with the grief that I often felt when I saw a child who, I knew, had only a few months to live, then these feelings would be reflected by a deterioration in our relationship. My own feelings very definitely helped or hindered the relationship and, in turn, my potential to help the child (Weininger, 1971).

This question of dealing with one's own feelings about the death of children is central to making hospitals more useful, more responsive, and more emotionally supportive for the dying child. Hospital staff need training and clinical supervision in order to work with these children. Far too often hospital staff feel impotent and angry that their medicines and forms of treatment do not cure the child. Often the anger is introjected by the child as a sense of doing or having done something bad or wrong. The staff's denial of death is witnessed when a child is taken out of the residential ward, out of the institutional hospital that the child has known for months or years, and brought to a strange ward in another hospital to die, now not attended by those he knew. The rationalization that was given to me was that "it will be easier for the child", or "There is more equipment in the other place", or "The other children will be very upset if the child died here." In my experience, the other children were indeed very upset at the death of a peer—but they expressed the concern that they wanted their friend to be with them, in the place they all knew. Some children took the staff's denial reaction over so completely that they simply denied that their friend had died, saying, "He's away on a vacation."

Some medical staff seem to have difficulty recognizing the limitations of their skills—they try so hard, and hope so much, and cannot accept failure even though it is not of their own making. They project these limitations onto the child by saying things like, "This medicine will make you feel better" or "You've been taking this medicine for a while now and you should be feeling better by now." It is almost as if the adult is commanding the child to get better, perhaps to compensate for the adult's own sense of failure or trying to "take control" of the illness and the child by a strong and suggestive element of adult authority. I think this adult reaction to the child's illness increases the child's sense of being "bad"—the child now senses that *he* has not responded to the "medicine" the proper way. One child of 9 years told me, "I cause only trouble because I can't get better" or "I'm trying to get better but nothing helps me." One young girl of 10 said, "Maybe they're giving me the wrong drugs, maybe they don't care what happens to me any more. I think they're fed up with me." If this occurs, the child's anxiety is increased and expressed as "being bad", "being in the way". The child wonders whether, if he died sooner, he would reduce the pressure he is creating on the medical staff and even on parents by not getting better. Perhaps, these children are also unable to respond to our ministrations. Their strong feelings may prevent the hospital treatment programme from being effective.

Melanie Klein (1940), writing about triumph, may encompass this physical reaction as well:

> Some people are obliged to remain unsuccessful because success [health] always implies to them the humiliation or even the damage of somebody else in the first place, the triumph over the parents, brothers and sisters. The efforts by which they seek to achieve something may be a highly constructive nature, but the implicit triumph and the ensuing harm and injury done to the object may outweigh these purposes in the subjects' mind and therefore prevent [health] their fulfilment. [Klein, 1940, p. 352]

At the same time, the child's willingness to verbalize his own anger and fear of dying is severely inhibited because it seems to the child that he has no right to be angry—only those people who are trying to help him and failing can be angry; "They're trying to help me, and I'm not helping myself", a 14-year-old girl said. This is certainly a very difficult situation for the child, the hospital staff, and the parents and often culminates in the child refusing to do things, becoming withdrawn, passively aggressive, sullen, or depressed, with bouts of expressed anger. While I was working with such children, I also discovered that they might not take their prescribed drugs. They may flush them down the toilet, or just "forget" to take them, or lose them in their room.

The emotions experienced as a consequence of feeling "I'm not doing all I can to help my medicine" must, I think, be given a safe opportunity to become expressed, to a person who can provide a feeling of security, even while the child is angry or sullen. The hospital staff with whom I have worked have had some difficulty with the anger the children have expressed and less so with the sullenness and depression. However, the wide range of children's feelings must be listened to and understood. Death is frightening to most children, but when the knowledge that "I'm going to die" is coupled with anger and depression, it is, I think, so much more difficult for the child to accept the containment some adults are trying to provide for them.

> The real source of the child's anxiety is his own aggressive wishes. It is largely allayed by his projecting the troublesome aggressive wishes on to an external object and so being afraid of it. The fear of this object is bad enough, but it is not so overwhelming as the internal anxiety and guilt it replaces. [Isaacs, 1933, p. 308]

I found that many hospital staff wanted to learn how to help the disabled or dying child, but often the "administration" stood in their way by not giving them enough time, by not encouraging their own growth, and, most unfortunately, by demanding that children behave "properly" rather than realizing the children's urgent need to express their feelings. The focus on maintaining the hospital as an institution (rather than a place where children live), where rules exist and flexibility seems to be very threatening, is extremely disheartening. I can recall the situation where some of the children, living in a hospital because of their very serious medical condition, wanted to put photographs of their family on the walls of their rooms. They were not allowed to do this because the walls would be damaged! Another incident happened when a few young girls wanted to grow their hair and were denied this opportunity. As one girl said, "My hair is the only thing that grows o.k. I have no trouble with my hair. I want it long." When the administration said that the staff do not have the time to wash "long hair", I told the "administration" that my students would help to wash the girl's hair, under the direction of nursing staff. However, the request was denied. Perhaps the rigidities of institutions exist as a method of coping with the unpredictabilities that expressive and affective human beings present. However, institutions must be made more understanding of children's needs and more truly responsive to their needs.

It is obviously extremely difficult to work daily with sick and dying children. Perhaps this is because we are afraid of the "unknown" of death and we have such a need for mastery and control, especially over the unknown. But by institutionalizing death, by denying the emotions that surround the dying child, we have tried to make it less a part of life—we have made death something to fight against to the bitter end and at all costs, rather than something we should accept as natural, as much a part of living as being born. Certainly we must try to provide all children with the best environment for living, but we must also recognize when we must provide the best environment for dying. Death, like birth, has to be something we can talk about with children, and must let them express their questions, fears, and anger. It may be difficult for many adults to recognize anger as a major component of their reaction to the death of someone they love or to their own imminent death. As a result, many parents feel the need to shield children from the reality of death, creating elaborate fantasies (Cornelison, 1976) and/or colourful euphemisms to evade the issue (Krasnow, 1992; Wenestam, 1984). It often does not feel right, somehow, to be angry at someone because they have died and have abandoned you, or to be angry because you will not be able to do, or be, or share in life any longer yourself, or because you cannot protect your child "physically or emotionally from want, pain and fear" (Bluebond-Langner, 1978, p. 214). Parents become very upset by their loss of authority and control over what is happening to their young (p. 215).

Glaser and Strauss (1965) point out that "some physicians purposely specialize in branches of medicine that will minimize their chances of encountering dying patients. Many nurses frankly admit preference for wards or fields where there is little confrontation with death and where people get better" (p. 240). Physicians are also "used to the feelings of authority and control" (Bluebond-Langner, 1978, p. 218), and perhaps anything less, especially in the face of death, creates a feeling of anger, or at least of impotence.

It is, I think, the difficulty we have in accepting our own anger about death that makes it so difficult for many of us to accept the anger of children. However, as professionals in institutions that exist for disabled and dying children, both individually and in groups, we must in fact begin to accept the total range of human emotions. We must commit ourselves to providing opportunities for children to recognize fully their own humanity, to affirm their likeness to all other human beings, whatever their physical condition may be, to live as fully as possible, whatever span of time we can medically provide for them, and to die with as little fear as possible and as much sense of our love and protection as we can extend to them. Every child must have our commitment to provide all the help we can give. The child must also have our emotional containment and psychological guidance to affirm an inalienable right as a human being to have feelings and to express them freely.

Children have to take in our love and nurturance to survive, but some children cannot do this. Their wish to be well and healthy seem to have become, not unnaturally, so fierce that they experience a

> defiance and aggression in connection with this wish [which gives] rise to the utmost anxiety of having everything taken from oneself, and thus being utterly destroyed. Not only so, it will then carry with it the dread of destroying the source of good by the act of taking. [Isaacs, 1933, p. 316]

While "many children meet this situation by building up the hope of giving back, . . . what has been taken so as to make her [mother] better again and thus make oneself better again" (p. 316), the dying child is not able to do this. This child's impending death has made "everyone" upset and "even angry" and these children experience this projected anxiety and feel "utterly destroyed" (p. 316). They have no capacity to take in goodness or to hold it for themselves if they do take in. They need a continuous containing person and a containing setting that will help them to express and to understand their internal world better (Klein, 1940) and help them cope not only with the sense of danger, if not terror, of their own death, but the danger they phantasize they are putting others to (Isaacs, 1948).

CHAPTER THIRTEEN

"Our minds help create the world we think we inhabit" [Piercy, 1991]

The world we live in is a world of images, and babies experience this internal world as the image of being safe and free of discomfort. The image is of a good internal object—one that contains the anxieties of fearfulness. The image is built up from the very early experiences of being contained or not being contained, and while the capacity to imagine or to phantasize is present at birth, it is always under the influence of the outside world—the world that parents and caregivers create for their babies. The baby's emotional response, as a consequence of being comforted or being discomforted, of being pleased or being angry, is incorporated within the phantasy. This incorporation determines the way the baby will react and respond to the external object. I think this response takes place at first in phantasy within the visual–somatic experiences of the baby. The baby responds, and then the nature of the real interaction with the external parents and caregivers takes place. If this interaction calms the baby, then the phantasy of being nurtured, of being comforted, of being supported by an internal object of goodness is strengthened. If this interaction is inadequate or discomforting, then the visual–somatic phantasy is of being in pain and of being destroyed. The phantasy then is to try to survive, and this is accomplished by projection. The object is subsequently phantasized as being damaged, and the ensuing interaction is painful and discomforting, probably for both baby and parent. The consequence is a withdrawal from the interaction by the baby and a sense of confusion and frustration by the parent. As the parent tries to continue with care for the baby, without recognizing the quality of the interaction, the baby can only respond with the phantasy that this is retaliation for its anger and projection. And the baby's world continues to be discomforting and bad. The fear then becomes one of being destroyed and annihilated at the hands of what can now be felt as a persecutor. This parent continues to care for the baby but does not recognize or realize that the baby experiences the care as noxious.

To avoid destruction, annihilation, and death, the baby may project the destruction to the external object as well as against parts of its self—against the external object to stay alive and against the self for these attacks. The superego's harshness gives voice to the experienced fear forcing a withdrawal, a failure to thrive, or an unusual obedience, as if there were "no more fight left". This is, I think, what happens when patients talk about something so bad in themselves that they cannot think or talk about "it", and whenever they broach the topic, they feel "so dizzy" or "so weak", or even fall asleep. It is difficult for them to think or talk about these images and feelings, and this stops them from talking about "feeling good" or "feeling vital"—essentially, from talking about life. Perhaps they are also preventing themselves from becoming aware of their envious attacks against an object felt to have the "good stuff", which would make them feel safe, comfortable, and contained.

The good and the bad, the comfortable and the uncomfortable—these visual–somatic images must come together in normal development. This occurs when the parents and caregivers realize the difficulties within their interactions with the baby. They try to contain the anxieties, fears, and complaints of their baby, rather than simply pressing on to get the exchange finished because they have no time! The fusion of the good and the bad, the lessening of the quality of the projections and the continuing containing love and nurturing experiences of the baby enable the superego's harshness to subside, the voice of the death instinct to be lessened, and the relation with the good object to be strengthened and internalized. This empowers the person to endure some envy, some anger, and some grief, and to continue being.

REFERENCES

Abramson, J. B. (1986). Liberation and its limits: The moral and political thought of Freud. Boston, MA: Beacon Press.

Alford, C. F. (1989). *Melanie Klein and critical social theory.* New Haven, CT: Yale University Press.

Anthony, Z., & Bhana, K. (1988–89). An exploratory study of Muslim girls' understanding of death. *Omega, 19*: 215–227.

Becker, E. (1973). *The denial of death.* New York: The Free Press.

Bion, W. R. (1967). *Second thoughts.* London Heinemann [reprinted London: Karnac Books, 1984].

Bluebond-Langner, M. (1978). *The private world of dying children.* Princeton, NJ: Princeton University Press.

Childers, P., & Wainer, M. (1971). The concept of death in early childhood. *Child Development, 42*: 1299–1301.

Cornelison, G. (1976). *Death and childhood: Attitudes and approaches in society, children's literature and children's theatre and drama.* (Doctoral dissertation, University of Kansas, 1975.) Ann Arbor, MI: Xerox University Microfilms.

Crittenden, P. M. (1992). Treatment of anxious attachment in infancy and early childhood. *Development and Psychopathology, 4*: 575–602.

Crittenden, P. M. (in press). Peering into the black box: An exploratory treatise on the development of self in young children. In: D. Chicchetti & S. L. Toth (Eds.), *Rochester Symposium on Development and Psychopathology: Vol. 5—The self and its disorders*. Rochester, NY: University of Rochester Press.

Davis, G. L. (1986). A content analysis of fifty-seven children's books with death themes. *Child Study Journal, 16*: 39–54.

Eigen, M. (1995). On Bion's no-thing. *Melanie Klein and Object Relations, 13*: 31–36.

Emde, R. N., Gaesbauer, T. J., & Harmon, R. J. (1976). *Emotional expression in infancy: A biobehavioral study*. New York: International Universities Press.

Essa, E. L., & Murray, C. I. (1994). Young children's understanding and experience with death. *Young Children, 49*: 74–81.

Federn, P. (1932). The reality of the death instinct especially in melancholia. *Psychoanalytic Review, 19*: 129–151.

Fetsch, S. H. (1986). The 7-to-10-year-old child's conceptualization of death. *Oncology Nursing Forum, 11*: 52–56.

Fisher, S., & Fisher, R. L. (1993). *The psychology of adaptation to absurdity*. Hillsdale, NJ: Lawrence Erlbaum Associates.

Formanek, R. (1974). When children ask about death. *Elementary School Journal, 75*: 92–97.

Freud, S. (1923). *The ego and the id. Standard edition of the complete works of Sigmund Freud, Vol. 19*. London: Hogarth Press, 1975.

Friedman, S. B., Chodoff, P., Mason, J. W., & Hamburg, D. A. (1963). Behavioural observations on parents anticipating the death of a child. *Pediatrics, 32*: 610–626.

Fries, M. (1935). Interrelatedness of the physical, mental and emotional life of a child from birth to 4 years of age. *American Journal of Disturbed Children, 49* (6): 230–240.

Galdston, R., & Gamble, W. J. (1969). On borrowed time: Observations on children with implanted cardiac pacemakers and their families. *American Journal of Psychiatry, 126*: 104–108.

Gartley, W., & Bernasconi, N. (1967). A concept of death in children. *Journal of Genetic Psychology, 110*: 71–85.

Glaser, B., & Strauss, A. (1965). *Awareness of dying: A study of social interaction*. Chicago, IL: Aldene.

Goldy, F. R., & Katz, A. H. (1963). Social adaptation in hemophilia. *Children, U. S. Department of Health, Education and Welfare* (pp. 189–193).

Hansen, Y. (1972). *Development of the concept of death: Cognitive aspect.* Unpublished doctoral dissertation, California School of Professional Psychology, Los Angeles.

Heimann, P. (1952). Certain functions of introjection and projection in early infancy. In: M. Klein, P. Heimann, S. Isaacs, & J. Riviere (Eds.), *Developments in psycho-analysis* (pp. 122–168). London: Hogarth Press.

Hoffman, S. I., & Strauss, S. (1985). The development of children's concepts of death. *Death Studies, 9:* 469–482.

Isaacs, S. (1933). *Social development in young children: A study of beginnings.* London: Routledge & Kegan Paul.

Isaacs, S. (1948). The nature and function of phantasy. *International Journal of Psycho-Analysis, 29:* 73–97.

Joseph, B. (1982). Addiction to near death. *International Journal of Psycho-Analysis, 63:* 449–456.

Kastenbaum, R. (1965). The realm of death: An emerging area in psychological research. *Journal of Human Relations, 13:* 538– 552.

Klatt, H. J. (1991). In search of a mature concept of death. *Death Studies, 15:* 177–187.

Klein, M. (1933). The early development of conscience in the child. In: *Love, guilt and reparation and other works, 1921–1945* (pp. 248–257). London: Hogarth Press, 1975 [reprinted London: Karnac Books, 1992].

Klein, M. (1935). A contribution to the psychogenesis of manic-depressive states. In: *Love, guilt and reparation and other works, 1921–1945* (pp. 262–289). London: Hogarth Press, 1975 [reprinted London: Karnac Books, 1992].

Klein, M. (1940). Mourning and its relation to manic-depressive states. *Love, guilt and reparation and other works, 1921–1945* (pp. 344–369). London: Hogarth Press, 1975 [reprinted London: Karnac Books, 1992].

Klein, M. (1946). Notes on some schizoid mechanisms. In: *Envy and gratitude and other works, 1946–1963* (pp. 1–24). London: Hogarth Press, 1975 [reprinted London: Karnac Books, 1993].

Klein, M. (1955). The psycho-analytic play technique: Its history and significance. In: M. Klein, P. Heimann, & R. Money-Kyrle (Eds.), *New directions in psycho-analysis.* London: Tavistock [reprinted London: Karnac Books, 1985]. In: *Envy and gratitude and other works, 1946–1963* (pp. 122–140). London: Hogarth Press, 1975 [reprinted London: Karnac Books, 1993].

Klein, M. (1957a). Envy and gratitude. In: *Envy and gratitude and other works, 1946–1963* (pp. 176–235). London: Hogarth Press, 1975 [reprinted London: Karnac Books, 1993].

Klein, M. (1957b). *Envy and gratitude—A study of unconscious sources.* New York: Basic Books.

Klein, M. (1958). On the development of mental functioning. *International Journal of Psycho-Analysis, 39*: 84–90. In: *Envy and gratitude and other works, 1946–1963* (pp. 236–246). London: Hogarth Press, 1975 [reprinted London: Karnac Books, 1993].

Klein, M. (1959). Our adult world and its roots in infancy. *Human Relations, 12*: 291–303. In: *Envy and gratitude and other works, 1946–1963* (pp. 247–263). London: Hogarth Press, 1975 [reprinted London: Karnac Books, 1993].

Klein, M. (1969). Mourning and its relation to manic-depressive states. In: H. M. Ruitenbeek (Ed.), *Death: Interpretations* (pp. 237–267). New York: Dell.

Koocher, G. P. (1973). Childhood, death, and cognitive development. *Developmental Psychology, 9*: 369–375.

Koocher, G. P. (1974a). Conversations with children about death: Ethical considerations in research. *Journal of Clinical Child Psychology, 3*: 19–21.

Koocher, G. P. (1974b). Talking with children about death. *American Journal of Orthopsychiatry, 44*: 404–411.

Krasnow, J. E. (1992). *The impact of experience on children's conceptions of death.* Unpublished doctoral dissertation, State University of New York, Buffalo.

Lansdown, R. (1989). The care of the child fearing death. *Progress in Pediatric Surgery, 22*: 64–68.

Lanzi, G., Balottin, U., Borgatti, R., & Ottolini, A. (1993). Relational and therapeutic aspects of children with late onset of a terminal disease. *Child's Nervous System, 9*: 339–342.

Lazar, A., & Torney-Purta, J. (1991). The development of the subconcepts of death in young children: A short-term longitudinal study. *Child Development, 62*: 1321–1333.

Lewis, M. (1995). Self-conscious emotions. *American Scientist, 83*: 68–78.

Meltzer, D. (1968). Terror, persecution, dread—A dissection of paranoid anxieties. *International Journal of Psycho-Analysis, 49*: 396–401.

Mikulincer, M., Florian, V., & Tolmacz, R. (1990). Attachment styles and fear of personal death: A case study of affect regulation. *Journal of Personality and Social Psychology, 58*: 273–280.

Nagy, M. (1948). The child's theories concerning death. *Journal of Genetic Psychology, 73*: 3–27.

Noland, R. (1971). *Counselling parents of the ill and handicapped.* Springfield, Il: Charles C Thomas.

Orbach, I. (1988). *Children who don't want to live.* San Francisco, CA: Jossey-Bass.

Oster, H., & Ekman, P. (1978). Facial behavior in child development. *Minnesota Symposium in Child Psychology: Vol. 11* (pp. 213–276).

Papadatou, D. (1991). Working with dying children: A professional's personal journey. In: D. Papadatou & C. Papadatos (Eds.), *Children and death* (pp. 285–292). New York: Hemisphere Publishing Corporation.

Piaget, J. (1951). *The child's conception of physical causality.* London: Kegan Paul.

Piercy, M. (1991). *He, she and it.* New York: Fawcett Crest.

Raimbault, G. (1991). The seriously ill child: Management of family and medical surroundings. In: D. Papadatou & C. Papadatos (Eds.), *Children and death* (pp. 177–182). New York: Hemisphere Publishing Corporation.

Richards, J. B., & Waisman, H. A. (1955). Psychological aspects of management of children with malignant diseases. *American Journal of Diseases of Children, 89*: 42–47.

Rochlin, G. R. (1959). The loss complex: A contribution to the etiology of depression. *Journal of the American Psychoanalytic Association, 7*: 299–316.

Rosenfeld, H. (1964). On the psychopathology of narcissism. *International Journal of Psycho-Analysis, 45*: 332—337.

Rosenfeld, H. (1971). A clinical approach to the psycho-analytical theory of the life and death instinct: An investigation into the aggressive aspects of narcissism. *International Journal of Psycho-Analysis, 52*: 169–178.

Rosenfeld, H. A. (1990). *Impasse and interpretation: Therapeutic and anti-therapeutic factors in the psychoanalytic treatment of psychotic, borderline and neurotic patients.* London: Routledge.

Safir, G. (1964). A study in relationships between life and death in children. *Journal of Genetic Psychology, 105*: 283–295.

Saint-Cyr, L. (1994). *Aspects of the paranoid-schizoid and depres-*

sive positions—Special challenges and vulnerabilities of handi-capped infants. Unpublished paper, University of Toronto/O. I. S. E., Toronto.

Schonfeld, D. J., & Kappelman, M. (1990). The impact of school-based education on the young child's understanding of death. *Journal of Developmental and Behavioral Pediatrics, 11*: 249–252.

Segal, H. (1957). Notes on symbol formation. *International Journal of Psycho-Analysis, 38*: 211–224.

Segal, H. (1973). *Introduction to the work of Melanie Klein.* London: Hogarth Press.

Segal, H. (1993). On the clinical usefulness of the concept of the death instinct. *International Journal of Psycho-Analysis, 74*: 55–61.

Sparta, S. N. (1987). The professional's role in discussing death with seriously ill children and their families. In J. E. Schowalter (Ed.), *Children and death: Perspectives from birth through adolescence* (pp. 85–91). New York: Praeger.

Speece, M. W., & Brent, S. B. (1984). Children's understanding of death: A review of three components of a death concept. *Child Development, 55*: 1671–1686.

Sperling, O. E. (1948). On the mechanisms of spacing and crowding emotions. *International Journal of Psycho-Analysis, 29*: 232–235.

Spillius, E. B. (1994). Developments in Kleinian thought: Overview and personal view. *Psychoanalytic Inquiry, 14* (3): 324–364.

Spinetta, J. (1974). The dying child's awareness of death. *Psychological Bulletin, 81*: 256–260.

Stambrook, M., & Parker, K. C. (1987). The development of the concept of death in childhood: A review of the literature. *Merrill-Palmer Quarterly, 33*: 133–157.

Steiner, J. (1981). Perverse relationships between parts of the self: A clinical illustration. *International Journal of Psycho-Analysis, 62*: 241–251.

Suttie, I. D. (1935). *The origins of love and hate.* London: Kegan, Paul, Teuch & Truber.

Valenzuela, M. (1989). *Mother–infant attachment, developmental status and quality of home care in young chronically undernourished children.* Unpublished Ph.D. thesis, University of Toronto, Toronto, Canada.

van Eys, J. (1987). The definition of dying and the personhood of the child. In: J. E. Schowalter (Ed.), *Children and death: Perspective from birth through adolescents* (pp. 113–122). New York: Praeger.

Vianello, R., & Lucamante, M. (1988). Children's understanding of death according to parents and pediatricians. *Journal of Genetic Psychology, 149*: 305–316.

Weininger, O. (1971). Another way of looking at the intimate experience: Two case histories. *Involvement, 3*: 13–16.

Weininger, O. (1972). Effects of parental deprivation. An overview of the literature and report on some current research. *Psychological Reports, 30*: 591–612.

Weininger, O. (1975). The disabled and dying children: Does it have to hurt so much. *Ontario Psychologist, 1*: 29–35.

Weininger, O. (1979a). Young children's concepts of dying and dead. *Psychological Reports, 44*: 395–407.

Weininger, O. (1979b). *Play and education: The basic tool for early childhood learning.* Springfield, IL: Charles C Thomas.

Weininger, O. (1989). *Children's phantasies: The shaping of relationships.* London: Karnac Books.

Weininger, O. (1992). *Melanie Klein: From theory to reality.* London: Karnac Books.

Weininger, O. (1993). *View from the cradle: Children's emotions in everyday life.* London: Karnac Books.

Weiss, E. (1935). Todestrieb and masochismus. *Image, 21*: 393–411.

Wenestam, C.-G. (1984). Qualitative age-related differences in the meaning of the word "death" to children. *Death Studies, 8*: 333–347.

Wenestam, C.-G., & Wass, H. (1987). Swedish and U.S. children's thinking about death: A qualitative study and cross-cultural comparison. *Death Studies, 11*: 99–121.

Yule, V. (1979). *What happens to children: The origins of violence.* London: Robertson.

Zilboorg, G. (1943). Fear of death. *Psychoanalytic Quarterly, 12*: 465–475.

INDEX